Second

# The Secretary's Survival Manual

## Sandra Tomkins

KOGAN
PAGE

For John, who made it all possible

First published in 1986
Second edition 1991

Apart from any fair dealing for the purposes of research or private study, or criticism or review, as permitted under the Copyright, Designs and Patents Act, 1988, this publication may only be reproduced, stored or transmitted, in any form or by any means, with the prior permission in writing of the publishers, or in the case of reprographic reproduction in accordance with the terms of licences issued by the Copyright Licensing Agency. Enquiries concerning reproduction outside those terms should be sent to the publishers at the undermentioned address:

Kogan Page Limited
120 Pentonville Road
London N1 9JN

© Sandra Tomkins 1986, 1991

**British Library Cataloguing in Publication Data**

A CIP record for this book is available from the British Library.

ISBN 0-7494-0432-9

Typeset by DP Photosetting, Aylesbury, Bucks
Printed and bound in Great Britain by
Biddles Limited, Guildford and Kings Lynn

# Contents

# Introduction

In bygone days there was a certain prestige to secretarial work. Progression up the career ladder was a slow but steady climb from the lowly position of 'office junior' to the absolute pinnacle of 'personal secretary'.

The heady days of the 1960s put an end to all this. There was an acute shortage of secretaries – they could pick and choose from an abundance of jobs. Employment agencies mushroomed, and anyone who could type called themselves a secretary. Standards and expectations dropped, and the profession got a bad name. As a result, secretarial work was viewed as a 'last resort' in the 1970s by a more discriminating labour force who had not yet felt the pinch.

Happily, we seem to be coming full circle – and about time too. The growing sophistication of business practice and the advent of new technology during the 1980s have sharpened us all, and two recessions have eliminated the dead wood. Thankfully, the stereotyped 'office bimbo' is no longer painting her nails. Employers are more discerning, agencies more thorough and secretaries take a rightful pride in their profession. For a profession it is. A true PA is an executive in her own right with more responsibility than many managers – and let no one tell you otherwise.

Today it is important to remember that many secretaries are men, many bosses women, and the old subservient days have gone. We now have real teamwork without the dominance of either sex (well, usually).

Thanks to changing population patterns, economic pressures and more enlightened employment attitudes, the 1990s also look like being the decade of the mature, and often returning, secretary whose value has at last been appreciated.

The beauty of secretarial work is that it can be your passport into any sphere of business life, and by moving around selectively you will become not only more experienced in secretarial matters but extremely knowledgeable about business in general. The world really is your oyster.

There could be no better time than the 1990s to choose a secretarial career. Virtually all the old typewriter-bashing drudgery has disap-

7

peared with new technology and there are now more opportunities for the real challenge of secretarial work – that of being one step ahead of your boss. The well-trained and sensitive secretary is a unique asset – smoothing away problems and providing a tranquil base.

Secretarial work is never dull – I've been asked to type in Portuguese, find a client's colostomy bags and, with only one hour's notice, prepare a buffet meal for 20. This is the fun part of secretarial life (although it doesn't usually feel like it at the time) and coping cannot be learnt at college. Of course, the basics are essential – and you should master these before taking a secretarial post – but if, in addition, your boss has complete confidence in your overall abilities, you will have a relaxed and successful partnership. This is the real object of secretarial practice, which brings me to the point of this newly revised and updated book.

There are many short cuts to the knowledge normally gained by experience, and much information you may only need once to cope with your particular job. In the second edition of this book I have described many facets of office life so that you have a point of reference if something unfamiliar crops up in your secretarial day. If you are contemplating a secretarial career, reading through this book will give you an idea of its scope and perhaps convince you that it is not that last resort. If you are returning to a secretarial career, the expanded chapter on new technology will help to gen you up on the very latest developments and ease you back into the challenging business world of the 1990s. This section should also be helpful to established secretaries who may have concerns about the equipment itself or the dilemma of a changing role.

If you are interested in taking advantage of the unprecedented opportunities ahead for secretaries with the introduction of the Single European Market in 1992, I hope the new appendix on this fundamental change to modern working life will be useful.

Lastly, you may be glancing at this book if you're a boss, and maybe you too can learn something!

# Part 1: Making the Job Your Own

# Chapter 1

# A Plan for the Future

You are a versatile, quick-thinking professional and at 27 may be earning as much as £17,000 a year. You could qualify for a subsidised mortgage, non-contributory pension, BUPA, free lunches, clothing allowance and even a company car. In the 1990s the demand for career secretaries is growing and today's remuneration packages show just how highly employers rate their top PAs. Of course, to earn these salaries you will need to have at least five years' top-level experience and will probably work in the City of London. Nevertheless, salaries elsewhere for the well-qualified and experienced secretary do not fall that far behind and first-class conditions of employment can be commanded.

Open the classified section of *The Times* any Monday, Wednesday or Thursday and you will see ample evidence of the opportunities available for secretaries. There are all kinds of job openings with wildlife conservation societies, top-class international companies and even the odd (or very odd) millionaire.

The 1991 recession has affected all areas and at the present time there is strong competition for secretarial work.

However, secretarial employment prospects should improve with a more buoyant economy and once the anticipated fall in the number of school leavers has occurred. At that time there is likely to be a shortfall in the number of secretaries which could be met from the increasing number of mature people returning to work. Employment consultants Crone Corkill also believe that secretarial college leavers will be in particular demand once prospects improve.

Additionally, the advent of the Single European Market in 1992 should mean an enormous increase in jobs throughout the Community, especially for multilingual secretaries or those willing to learn other languages.

Secretarial agencies are therefore bracing themselves for the boom they feel is just around the corner. When unemployment looms over everyone's shoulder, it is reassuring to know that you are in a potential growth industry and will be well rewarded for your endeavours.

## What is a secretary?

This can best be summed up by saying that the more effective the secretary, the more productive the boss. By dealing with all routine and administrative matters a true PA enables her boss to concentrate on his proper job. What does this mean in real terms?

- By organising his day sufficiently well so that he can make the very best use of his working time (without being worn to a frazzle);
- By organising his priorities without becoming bossy;
- By using her judgement and initiative to deputise and handle problems when he is out of town;
- By screening him from unnecessary callers and problems, and thus saving his time;
- Conversely, by having the sense to bring important matters to his attention when necessary;
- By acting as a confidential sounding board when he's under pressure and/or needs to let off steam;
- By acting as a vital link between him and his staff so he does not get out of touch;
- By handling those trivial and unimportant details in his life which become very important when not dealt with properly.

It is sometimes difficult to appreciate just how complex is the role of the secretary because so many of her efforts are geared to making it look simple. Like the proverbial clock, it is only when it stops ticking that you can appreciate the number of moving parts.

What then makes the perfect secretary? You need to have sound basic skills – shorthand or speedwriting of at least 100 words per minute, and accurate typing of at least 50 words per minute. Audio typing is a popular form of text transcription, so don't turn your nose up at tapes. But don't forget your shorthand either. Funnily enough, many employers who have converted to audio still give shorthand as a requirement in advertisements, because it is seen as a characteristic in the best-quality applicants. Word processing is now seen as an absolute necessity by all but the smallest organisations. Ideally, you should have a working knowledge of two or three of the best-known software packages – Wang, Multimate, Word Perfect, Wordstar – but virtually all employers are willing to cross-train should this be necessary. More about technology skills in Chapter 9. All in all, we secretaries have to be more versatile than ever and need many technical strings to our bow.

What personal qualities will you need? I put a sense of humour right at the top of the list – when all else fails, a good laugh can usually get you out of a difficult or embarrassing situation. You need to be tolerant of everything and of bad language in particular. I once sent a highly confidential telex to the wrong client on behalf of my volatile Texan boss. As he'd warned me of the dire consequences should it fall into the wrong hands, I knew I was for it. He threw the offending documents at me, using words not found in an English (or American) dictionary. I stood rooted to the spot and when the bad language stopped, my contrite expression raised a smile all round. Had I uttered even one word, I don't think I'd be here today.

Resourcefulness and initiative are essential qualities. While my boss was in a remote part of the world not renowned for its communications, I received an urgent request for him to visit Brazzaville, visas for which could only be obtained from the Congolese Embassy in Paris. Before he had knowledge of the invitation, I sent the visa application to Paris via one of our staff making a journey there, and the authorised endorsement was back in my hands before my boss returned to the office. This bit of initiative saved me from a real panic on the one day he spent in London between trips, and reassured him that I did not spend all day at the hairdresser's when he was out of town.

I hate admitting it, but the best secretary needs to be a first-class fibber. All secretaries have to bend the truth at times on behalf of their boss who may not want to speak to an irate client, the bank manager or (worst of all) an ex-wife. Our sole comfort is that we secretaries tell white lies only as a last resort and they don't extend beyond the office.

You need to be methodical, hardworking and able to assess priorities. Hopping from one task to another haphazardly, and leaving those you dislike until last, will get you absolutely nowhere. All employers like to feel their business is being conducted efficiently. If you are good at juggling priorities logically, you will have a happy boss. Saving yourself from unnecessary problems and having a good relationship with your boss are the secret of successful secretarial work.

Many of the skills I've described can be cultivated and do come with experience. With judgement, common sense and a little luck, you'll find they become second nature.

As for my qualifications to write this book, I've been in secretarial work for 20 years, starting as junior shorthand typist and working up to board director's PA of a major international company. I have worked in professional, charitable and commercial organisations as a secretary and have also spent some time in personnel management. As well as my permanent jobs, I've had several spells of temporary work and hence have worked for many different people in my journey up the career ladder. Among other things I've been involved in the sale of a daily newspaper, have made tea and represented the firm abroad.

All the anecdotes in this book are true. I hope some make you laugh, and all of them show what secretarial work is really like.

## Interests, aims and objectives

First things first. You're looking for a secretarial job and need to formulate a career plan. Unless you're a 'flitter' by nature, it doesn't make sense to hop from one job to another without some clear purpose. With secretarial opportunities in so many fields, it pays to be selective.

Look at yourself first and list your strengths and weaknesses. There is no point in deciding on a secretarial career in a given field if you don't have the right qualities. Get someone who knows you well, but not emotionally, to look your list over and check your objectivity.

Having decided that secretarial work is for you, select your area(s) of interest. Perhaps you are drawn to the legal profession or television, or are enthralled by the medical scene? If you have no idea about your area of interest, it will help filter ideas to make a list of subjects you did well in at school and enjoyed; what captures your imagination; what you have staying power for. It's also worth noting down subjects you definitely don't like so these can be excluded from your final selection. Ask yourself the following questions:

- Do I have a social 'bent'? (*hospitals, social work, education, charities*);
- Am I attracted by big business or the professions?
- Do I want to travel? (*Diplomatic Service, big banks, World Health Organisation, EC, United Nations, travel companies, airlines*);
- Do I like glamour? (*advertising, PR, photography*);
- Do I prefer routine? (*Civil Service, accountancy, legal profession, banking*);
- Do I like peaks and troughs in my work pattern? (*management consultancies, advertising*).

Working in your chosen field (once you've discovered it) can make all the difference to your secretarial career.

When you have an idea of your area of interest, you need to decide on your career goal. Do you want to be the managing director's PA or do you prefer the camaraderie of a secretarial team? Ask yourself some more questions:

- How ambitious am I?
- Am I a nine-to-fiver whose job is a means to an end?
- Am I in good health and able to cope with the physical demands of my job?
- Do I have a spouse and family to consider?
- Am I prepared to travel?
- Do I want to use a foreign language?
- Do I want to use my secretarial job as a stepping stone to an executive position?

- Am I a one-boss person, or happiest in a team?
- Could I work for someone of the same sex?

Try to be as objective as possible about what is feasible and practical. You can hardly become an MD's PA when you've just left college, but it's always good to have a long-term goal. There's no better way of gaining experience than by gradually working your way up the career ladder. You'll give yourself confidence and show future employers that you really mean business.

However, if you are unsure that secretarial work is for you, have no idea of your area of interest, or want to move from secretarial work into management, then the Vocational Guidance Association can help set you straight. Their advice service, which has been around for 37 years, is based on a series of personality, interest and aptitude tests which take half a day to complete. These tests are normally held at the London head office but there are also regional facilities throughout the UK. Test results are interpreted by an experienced consultant during an in-depth discussion which lasts about one and a half hours. The consultation is geared to meeting individual needs and concentrates on particular circumstances, identifying strengths and weaknesses and discussing how these can be used to achieve job satisfaction. Recommendations are then made about the most appropriate career move.

The cost of VGA's service is £245 plus VAT which includes a written report detailing test results and summarising discussions with the consultant. There is also a two-year follow-up service in case further advice or help is needed.

For further details contact: The Vocational Guidance Association, 7 Harley House, Upper Harley Street, London NW1 4RP; tel 071-935 2600/071-486 2338; fax 071-486 4613.

**Secretarial case study**
In 1980 Wendy Syer accepted the position of director's secretary at Abbey National expecting to find the finance world a little stodgy and boring. Eleven years on, and now secretary to Sir Campbell Adamson, the Abbey's Chairman, she has to admit that she was wrong.

Sir Campbell is well known in industrial and government circles and was Director General of the CBI during the 1970s. He is also committed to industry working with charity and is Chairman of the Help the Aged Industry Appeals Committee, the Independent Broadcasting Telethon Trust and the Family Policy Studies Centre as well as being a governor of Rugby School. Consequently, no two days of Wendy's working life are ever the same.

What personal qualities does Wendy need in coping with her

particular job? First, the qualities needed by all secretaries at whatever level – patience, unflappability, boundless energy and a sense of humour. Wendy sees senior secretaries as being the keepers of all knowledge – of their company, their boss's myriad contacts, the allied industries, timetables, reference books, *et al.* If a secretary doesn't know the answer she must know where she can get it! (This aspect of secretarial work is considered in Chapter 7.) To this must be added the ability to appreciate the day's priorities without being told and to act accordingly: the silent communication between boss and secretary becomes paramount at senior level.

Although many secretaries acting at Wendy's level are fortunate enough to have an assistant, Wendy works single-handed and this can mean many long, hard days. The Abbey National converted from a building society to a public limited company in 1989 and this has also led to an increase in workload and additional pressure as the company has strived to become even more successful in its new role.

What about the impact of new technology? Nowadays all senior secretaries at Abbey National have computers linked via a local area network. Wendy can also tap into all main administration sites allowing fast exchange of information and she works with a variety of word processing and computer programs. Virtually the whole of her working day is stored electronically in the equipment on her desk. The telephones and fax machines are programmed to dial numbers in the UK and abroad at the touch of a button, re-dialling automatically as necessary. Wendy thinks it is almost impossible to assess how much time and effort is saved having so much information and technology to hand while working from one desk. (Chapter 9 considers the impact of new technology on secretarial work.)

Although her working days are so different, Wendy does try to follow the routine she learnt during her first job back in the 1960s. First, she scans the newspapers. As she says, 'You have to know what is going on in your own and allied industries.' Then she opens and sorts the post, opens Sir Campbell's office, ensures papers for the day are to hand and checks her own priorities. As the pace hots up she tries to deal with filing from the previous day. Once the phone really gets going it is a question of juggling appointments and meetings, making travel arrangements and keeping everyone happy – including those who do not actually get to see Sir Campbell.

There are many calls and letters from customers every day which Wendy reviews carefully. She investigates major problems personally, drafting a reply for Sir Campbell to sign once the matter is resolved.

Although Sir Campbell's job does not generally necessitate Wendy travelling with him, she accompanied him during the publicity roadshows of 1989 when Abbey National was publicising its conversion to a plc. She also makes time each year to visit different Abbey National high street branches, regional offices and various departments within the company's many administration blocks to keep up to date with what is happening and to meet the many new people who are joining the company. She feels strongly that secretaries can never know too much about their business or the world at large.

The pay and conditions at the top of the finance industry are extremely good. Staff at Abbey National are paid competitive rates, with increases based on personal performance and bonuses if the company out-performs its set budget targets. There is also a good pension scheme, subsidised meals and mortgages, special schemes for women returning to work and for people wishing to take extended leave. They also have a gym and a resident nurse! And there are ample opportunities for further development and training.

Wendy's main work-related extra-mural activity is the European Association of Professional Secretaries. Membership is open to all secretaries who have worked for a minimum of three years at Chairman or Chief Executive level and there are 1400 members throughout the 15 European countries. In the last five years Wendy has been PR officer in the UK and is now the Executive PRO for the whole of Europe. She has travelled to many of the major European capitals during the past five years and is looking forward to seeing more during her term of office. She feels strongly that women in business must create networks to assist them with their job and that EAPS does just that. For more information about EAPS contact: Janis Nowak (UK PRO), Schroders plc, 120 Cheapside, London EC2V 6DS.

## Advice for college leavers

When asked about college leavers, employers commonly complain that too many of them run before they can walk. While it is obviously essential to have sound basic skills, a string of secretarial certificates is not an instant passport to a high-flying role. People and situations in real offices are a million miles away from those encountered in textbooks, and learning how to cope takes time. There is far more to secretarial work than meets the eye.

At 17, with only one year's work experience, I was given my first PA job by a company who were too mean to pay for someone with proper experience. I was thrilled to sit in my own office and answer the phone for my director boss. Alas, this was about all I could do. I blundered through the multitude of tasks before me and burst into tears with such regularity that my boss kept a supply of chocolate in his desk drawer with which to stem the flow. After months of misery and ineptitude, things began to improve, but it was a good year before the penny really dropped.

With hindsight, I now see that it would have been far better to have got a less responsible job in a more supportive environment at that stage of my career. Although there is much to be said for learning the hard way, your confidence and reputation can suffer immeasurably in the process.

I am not alone in this view. Angela Paterson, Trusthouse Forte's human resource executive, also advises college leavers to get sound junior secretarial experience. She sees too many would-be secretaries who have high job and salary expectations but little to offer an employer apart from mechanical skills.

She was, however, impressed by one 19-year-old applicant who had deliberately spent two years as a junior secretary in her first job. While not ideal, this job had provided good office experience necessary for career progression and showed on her CV that increasingly rare quality – staying power. If you set your career off on these lines you could find yourself PA to a main board director by the age of 27 – with salary and perks to match. Scrimp on the basics and you could be relegated to mediocrity for ever.

## Ideas into action

Now that you have an idea of your area of interest and career goal, read up about your chosen business. Making sure you have a good understanding of what is really involved will save you many disappointments later on. For example, some people are attracted to the reputed glamour of the advertising world. While there are undoubtedly some fun jobs to be had with extrovert characters, advertising can be a hard, thankless slog, and as mundane as the next job.

Read all the trade magazines of your preferred industry, or better still, talk to someone who is already involved. Write down the pros and cons, and decide if this is really for you. Once you're sure in your own mind, it's time to get fixed up.

*Chapter 2*

# Getting Fixed Up

## Temporary work as your way in

The jobs I've been happiest in have always started as temporary assignments through an employment agency. Although many temp jobs cover overload situations, holidays and sickness, many are unfilled vacancies. The wonderful thing about this method of job search is that you can try out the boss and the firm without commitment. Both parties can get to know each other realistically and if it doesn't work out, there's always another temp job.

I once temped for an ultra fussy executive while he looked for a new secretary. After three months of painstaking interviews, he was still without a secretary, and I ended up with the job myself. I'm sure we wouldn't have picked each other at a conventional interview but having worked together for some time, things just fell into place.

If some of your temporary assignments cover holidays and sickness, you can gain a valuable insight into the kind of job you may aspire to. You might fill in on a job at a particularly high level and see at first hand what it's like at the top. If temping for any length of time, you're likely to work for all manner of organisations which will help to identify your preferred environment.

If you're returning to secretarial work, then a spell of temporary assignments will help to restore your confidence and show you how today's business world has changed. With the flexibility of temping hours, you can ease yourself back into full-time work – if you have a family to consider – over a period of time.

I would recommend a spell of temping for most experienced people either as an exercise in itself, or as a preferred method of job search. I know no better way of finding what you really want.

## The conventional approach

The literal meaning of curriculum vitae is 'course of life' and a concise account of yours is absolutely essential in your search for the right job. No one looks less employable than an applicant who stares vacantly at the ceiling trying to remember details for an application form. A carefully

19

thought-out and well-presented CV puts you streets ahead of applicants like these.

If you haven't prepared a CV before, it's a good idea to make a rough version first. As you can see from the specimen on page 22, there are four main sections to be covered:

## 1. Personal details

- Name;
- Address;
- Telephone numbers: home and business (if convenient);
- Date of birth and *age* (it's surprising how many personnel officers can't work these out);
- Marital status, and number of children (if applicable).

You don't have to give your nationality unless a work permit is needed.

## 2. Education and qualifications

Begin with your secondary education and work forwards to any further education. Give the name(s) and address(es), of school/college/university, together with dates of attendance. Underneath each establishment show the examinations sat, grades achieved and when. Give details of any subsequent training, courses and spells with the armed forces.

## 3. Career history

Always begin with your most recent employer and work back chronologically, giving:

- Name, address and business of your employer;
- Name and position of your immediate boss;
- Your job title and a résumé of responsibilities;
- Dates of employment;
- Current salary (most recent job only);
- Reasons for leaving.

Always try to make your reason for leaving sound positive. If you're leaving because you hate your boss don't say so, even if it's true. Adopt something lofty – for instance, 'To find a more challenging opportunity'. I'm not suggesting you tell outright lies – it's just a question of showing yourself in the most favourable light. These days everybody has to do it.

## 4. Hobbies

Personnel officers always set great store by this section! Never be tempted, as I was years ago, to embroider on the hobbies section. Thinking that 'reading' sounded a bit boring, I added some interesting activities I'd only dabbled in. A personnel officer who obviously founded the ecology movement, pounced on my all-embracing hobby of 'conservation' and called my bluff in seconds! Thereafter I stuck to reading.

Don't be tempted to fill your CV with unnecessary information but do capitalise on your very real achievements. You are trying to whet an employer's appetite after all. Perhaps you've organised a conference single-handed, been awarded a bonus for special effort, or worked for someone unusual?

If you're applying for a first job, demonstrate your motivation in studies and life in general. Ask yourself these questions:

- Have I done a Saturday/holiday job?
- Have I done any voluntary work?
- Do I belong to any special organisations – Guides, Scouts, Greenpeace etc?
- Have I taken part in the Duke of Edinburgh's Award Scheme?
- Have I been involved in school activities – debating society, bridge club, school plays?
- Have I organised any activities myself?

The answers should help you to write a few lucid sentences to show you're someone a bit special.

If you are returning to work after a break, show your achievements while you've been away. Nothing looks worse on a CV than a big gap. If you've been busy having a family, say so and be proud of it. Perhaps you've organised a play group, been involved with the PTA, or become a dab hand at decorating. All this looks good and positive. Have you brushed up on your old skills with a refresher course? Perhaps you've taken the bull by the horns and learnt about word processors and computers (more about training for these in Chapter 9)? If you have used your initiative (and you must have done or you wouldn't have bought this book), make sure your potential employer knows about it.

However, never be tempted to make false claims on a CV. It's a short cut to nowhere and will get you nothing but a bad reputation.

Show the rough CV to someone who doesn't know your life history. Can they readily understand your 'course of life' and are they sufficiently impressed to want to know more? Once you feel happy with the rough, spend as long as it takes typing it to perfection or get a typing bureau to produce an impeccable copy. Check the final version carefully – it's surprisingly easy for errors to slip through when you're dealing with familiar subject matter.

If you really can't face tackling a CV yourself there are professionals to do it for you. Local and national daily papers generally carry several advertisements for CV production services. One such is Faculty CVs who will study your work experience and prepare a CV presenting this in the best possible light. They offer either a postal service by questionnaire or an Executive Service which includes two consultations, full careers advice and tactical approaches to career planning. Their charges are fairly high compared to many other CV production services but according to Michael Fisher their emphasis is on creating a document that markets the individual rather than reproducing personal details in a smart format. He also believes that people are unable to be objective about themselves and rarely write an accurate appraisal of their skills and expertise.

The 1991 charges of Faculty CVs are £80.00 for the postal service by questionnaire (£50.00 to students/undergraduates) and £150.00 for the Executive Service. Individual letters of application and mailshot letters can also be provided. For further details contact: Faculty CVs 12 Eccleston Square, London SW1P 7NP; tel 071-233 5560/5561; fax 071-233 5557.

Whichever way your CV has been prepared, get some pristine photocopies and you're all set for the job search.

## Specimen CV

### Curriculum Vitae

| | | | |
|---|---|---|---|
| Miss Amanda N Other | | D.O.B. | 1.1.56 |
| 1 Any Street | | Age | 35 |
| Anytown AN1 1TO | | Unmarried – no children | |

071-000 0000 (home)
071-111 1111 X 22 (business)

*Current skills*

| | |
|---|---|
| Shorthand | 100 wpm |
| Typewriting | 60 wpm |
| Audio | 75 wpm |
| Word processing | (give make of machine/package) |

*Education and qualifications*

| | | | |
|---|---|---|---|
| Any School for Girls | | 1967 – 1973 | |
| Anytown AN1 1TO | | | |
| GCE A Levels | English language | B | 1973 |
| | Mathematics | C | 1973 |
| GCE O Levels | English language | B | 1971 |

|  | Mathematics | B | 1971 |
|---|---|---|---|
|  | Sociology | C | 1971 |
|  | History | C | 1971 |
|  | English literature | D | 1971 |
| CSE | Commerce | 2 | 1971 |
|  | Geography | 3 | 1971 |

Any Secretarial College                                    1973 – 1975
Anytown AN1 1TO

Secretarial Studies Certificate:                        1975
        Background to business
        Communication – use of English
        Office procedures
        Communication – audio typing duties
        Word processing

| Pitmans | Typewriting elementary |  | 1974 |
|---|---|---|---|
|  | Typewriting advanced |  | 1975 |
|  | Shorthand | 80 wpm | 1975 |
|  | Shorthand | 90 & 100 wpm | 1975 |

*Courses*

Word processing (WordPerfect) two days 1983
Word processing (Multimate Adv II) two days 1989

*Career history*

- **ANY COMPANY LTD**          (UK holding company for international
  3 Any Street                          group with interests in property and metals)
  Anytown AN1 1TO

  SECRETARY/PA to GROUP MARKETING DIRECTOR (Mark Eastman) –
  1986/present

  SALARY: £16,000 per annum + subsidised mortgage

  RESPONSIBILITIES:

  - Organising annual overseas marketing conference and attending this as
    administrative co-ordinator;
  - Arranging overseas business trips;
  - Deputising for boss in his absence abroad;
  - Co-ordinating with PR consultancy;
  - Organising client meetings and presentations;
  - Conducting preliminary research and statistics.

  REASON FOR LEAVING: Having been in this job for five years, I am now
  ready for a new challenge – possibly overseas.

- **ANY OTHER COMPANY INC**          (London office of New York-based
  4 Uptown Street                              advertising agency)
  Uptown UP1 1TO

SECRETARY/PA to CREATIVE DIRECTOR (Giles Meredith) – 1982/1986

RESPONSIBILITIES:

- Production of client reports and presentations;
- Liaising between photographers and artists;
- Booking models and arranging props;
- Maintenance of photographic library.

REASON FOR LEAVING: When my American boss returned to head office, I decided to consolidate my advertising experience by obtaining a job in marketing.

- ANY & ANY COMPANY LTD        (Small local advertising agency)
  2 Downtown Street
  Downtown DO1 1TO

SECRETARY to ACCOUNT EXECUTIVE (Susanna Smith) – 1977/1982

RESPONSIBILITIES:

- Shorthand/typing and usual secretarial duties;
- Liaising between clients;
- Arranging meetings and presentations.

REASON FOR LEAVING: After five happy years, I was ready for a more senior secretarial job.

- ANY COMPANY & PTNRS        (Small firm of solicitors)
  41 Downtown Street
  Downtown DO1 1TO

JUNIOR SECRETARY/SHORTHAND TYPIST – 1975/1977

RESPONSIBILITIES:

- Shorthand/typing for the senior secretary;
- Running errands and photocopying;
- Post and stationery.

REASON FOR LEAVING: This job gave me a sound basis in secretarial work but after two years I wanted to try and obtain a job in advertising.

HOBBIES
Reading, cinema, theatre, cookery.

REFERENCES
Available on request.

## Sources of jobs

The most prestigious source of secretarial jobs is 'La Crème de la Crème' section in *The Times*, published every Monday, Wednesday and Thursday. They also have an 'Executive Crème' section on Wednesdays for senior PA and secretarial vacancies. While most of the jobs advertised are for the Central London area, jobs in other parts of the UK and overseas do appear fairly regularly.

The *Guardian* has a secretarial recruitment page on Mondays which has some emphasis on the arts, and there is a back-up page on Thursdays.

If you live in London, three magazines, *Girl About Town, Ms London* and *9 to 5*, containing office job advertisements, are handed out free at British Rail and London underground stations on weekdays.

*Memo* and *2000*, the monthly Pitman shorthand magazines, carry some job advertisements towards the end of an academic term but the bulk of space is taken by employment agencies.

The local newspaper, wherever you live, is always a good source of jobs.

Look in the trade magazine of the industry which interests you and see if there are any secretarial jobs advertised. The trade magazine of the advertising business, *Campaign*, often has some real beauties.

Magazines such as *Time Out, City Limits* and *New Statesman* often have slightly off-beat jobs for the secretary with a mission.

Having spotted a job, handwrite a businesslike letter, enclosing your CV and explaining why the vacancy appeals to you. Use short, clear sentences and don't waffle. The personnel officer will have a mound of applications to wade through. Use a pen and make sure your writing is legible. Only type your letter as a last resort; the employer wants to see your handwriting. A typed letter should not look as if it was dashed off when the boss's back was turned but should show your skill at layout.

Good-quality stationery is a sound investment – appearances are everything at this stage. Check your letter carefully for punctuation and spelling. This sounds like stating the obvious but several personnel officers complained to me about the dreadful presentation of application letters and the appalling spelling.

If you're not available for interview on a specific day, it is sensible to say so when making your application, but try not to be insistent that an interview should be totally at your convenience. Always be straightforward and reasonable in your dealings with potential employers.

## Writing on spec

This method of job search has two distinct advantages:

1. It allows you the freedom to research your area of interest and select organisations which best meet your criteria;
2. The company may gain by saving the cost of expensive advertising if you happen to write when a vacancy is in the offing (assuming you are a first-class candidate, of course). They should also be impressed by your motivation.

How do you track down the ideal company? You may select companies on the basis of their advertisements because you like the public image they project. Alternatively, make a trip to your local reference library and go through the yearbook of your chosen field. If you are interested in commerce, Dun and Bradstreet's *Key British Enterprises* gives good basic information. Some other useful yearbooks are listed in Chapter 7.

Otherwise enlist the aid of your librarian. From the basic facts you will be able to make a catalogue of those companies of broad interest. Obtain a copy of their annual report details by contacting the company direct, or checking with Companies House (details of how to obtain this information can be found in Chapter 7). From this more detailed data you can draw up a short list and write your letters of application.

Handwrite a brief letter explaining why you are sufficiently interested in their company to write on the off-chance. Enclose your CV and a stamped addressed envelope – as your application hasn't been requested you should always show the courtesy of an SAE.

Despite the advantages of this method, be prepared for a pile of rejections. Some companies may not even reply at all. For every 20 letters you write, there may be only one interview. Still, one interview may be all it takes to get the right job for you. You have nothing to lose, after all – good luck!

## Employment agencies

During the boom period of the 1960s and 1970s employment agencies had a field day. There was real money to be made and many adopted a hard sell approach in the scramble for business. To be fair, many applicants were spoilt for choice and treated the agencies badly, playing one off against another. As a result, placements from employment agencies were sometimes a hit and miss affair, and their reputation took a dive.

The recessions of the early 1980s and 1990s taught everyone a valuable lesson and both applicants and agencies became far more professional in their approach. The big agency chains have made a conscious effort to adopt more thorough procedures for matching applicants to jobs. There is also more competition from small, specialist agencies, who attracted many top-class candidates towards the end of the boom period in the late 1970s. Crone Corkill is a prime example of a specialist agency, with branches in the West End and City of London. They focus on high-powered permanent and temporary jobs for the career secretary, and on jobs with potential for college leavers. Although they have always handled language vacancies, the enormous increase in both jobs and candidates with the advent of 1992 has resulted in their setting up a separate Multilingual Division. They are thoroughly professional in their dealings with clients and concentrate on the individual strengths of each applicant. Because their consultants are not paid on a commission basis their advice to candidates is always objective and impartial. For further details contact: Crone Corkill & Associates Ltd, Victory House, 99–101 Regent Street, London W1R 7HB; 071-434 4512; fax 071-437 9239. Crone Corkill also have an office at 18 Eldon Street, London EC2M 7LA; 071-588 3535.

How can you decide which employment agency to use? If you live in a rural area you may well have Hobson's choice, but if you are based in a city, particularly London, you may not know which way to turn.

The Federation of Recruitment and Employment Services produces an annual directory which includes their 400 secretarial agency members, based throughout the UK. All Federation members are thoroughly vetted and have to abide by a code of conduct on professional standards. If an applicant has a complaint against a member agency, this will be fully investigated by the Federation. However, Christine Little, the Federation's deputy director, told me that they receive very few complaints probably because members are vetted in advance. Serious misdemeanours resulting in expulsion of members are extremely rare.

For further information contact: The Federation of Recruitment and Employment Services Ltd, 36–38 Mortimer Street, London W1N 7RB; tel 071-323 4300; fax 071-255 2878.

Having selected an agency, what kind of service should you expect? All agency applicants should have an in-depth interview with a trained consultant, and a test of mechanical skills, which will culminate in a carefully presented CV. If you find this kind of professional service is lacking, Christine's advice is to try elsewhere.

Try to keep a few days free for your job search. There is nothing worse than dashing into agencies in your lunch hour and cramming in the odd interview when you can. In such rushed conditions you will hardly create the best impression.

Having decided on the level you wish to pitch yourself, dress accordingly. If you're aiming to be a top PA put on something smart even if your favourite outfit is pink and punk. You have to look worth the job and in keeping with your professional image, even if this doesn't bear any relation to the 'real' you. Have your hair done and make sure you really look your best.

Most agencies are very informal and will call you by your first name. Remember it's in their interests to find you a job you'll stay in (their commission works that way), so you have them on your side. How can you get the very best from your employment agency? Christine Little recommends that you think over your job plans carefully before seeing a consultant. Be confident about your skills and experience but honest about any shortcomings. By adopting a professional attitude you will get the very best from those trying to help with your job search.

Having discussed your career plans, the agency will probably have some potential openings for you. Make sure you get as many real details as possible. The agency will have visited the firm if they have done their homework properly, and should be able to give you a good picture of what is on offer. Is the journey reasonable for you? Is the salary acceptable? Agencies will sometimes push jobs at lower salaries and suggest that the firm may increase its offer at an interview. Never be tempted. These kinds of interview are time-wasters for everybody.

Once you've identified some really suitable vacancies, the agency will submit your CV for consideration. This may take a bit of time, but is well worth it in the long run. With so much more information about you than a quick phone call, personnel officers are in a better position to assess your suitability. If called for an interview on this basis, you know you're in with a chance.

Try to have interviews arranged for the time of day when you are at your best. This is at 9.00 am for me but I'm probably in a minority.

## Interview and selection methods

When called for an interview, it's time well spent to research the company before you go. Get hold of the annual report details (see Chapter 7) and check on the company's solvency. There is nothing more depressing than joining an organisation which is going through a bad patch - you'll wish you'd never heard of them.

Make sure you know the exact interview location and precisely how to get there. If you can have a 'dry run' to time your journey so much the better, and allow extra time on the day itself. You're bound to be feeling a bit keyed up so try to avoid anything which causes extra stress - like arriving by the skin of your teeth. Wash your hair the night before, or have it done professionally, and make sure your outfit is immaculate.

First impressions at an interview are extremely important, says Angela Paterson, Trusthouse Forte's human resource executive, and applicants who take pride in their presentation, particularly in appearance and manner, inspire confidence in their ability to do the job. This is sound advice.

On interview day, try to get out of bed on the right side. A warm bath will relax and freshen you. If you can face eating, treat yourself to a special breakfast. Pampering yourself a bit will put you in a good mood and the day will go with a swing. If you feel like going to the interview by taxi, it's money well spent.

Your initial screening interview will probably be with the personnel officer. Take along your CV and be prepared to fill in an application form. This may seem a bore if you've already sent in a CV but most firms need a signed application form for their records. There is bound to be a health section and it's a good idea to have a note of any serious illnesses or operations you may have had during the past five years. Some firms also like to know how many days' sickness you have had in the previous year, so keep a record of these too. Giving incorrect information on an application form can be grounds for dismissal, so always be honest about any health problems you may have had.

Be prepared to do a skills test. These are not always given, particularly for senior jobs, but it's as well to expect the worst. Always take your time over a test and remember that accuracy is more important than speed. Personnel officers make allowances for the stress situation and unfamiliar equipment, so don't worry if the test doesn't match your usual standards. Just do the best you can.

Some companies, particularly American ones, may ask applicants to undertake intelligence and/or personality tests. Intelligence tests measure mental aptitude and are mainly used to gauge trainability. They usually take the form of questions based on letters, words and numbers, to which certain people rattle off the right answers in seconds flat. However, some psychologists think that good IQ test scores are more likely to prove quickness on the uptake rather than actual intelligence level – so don't despair if you don't score well.

Personality tests aim to measure interpersonal skills, but these are extremely subjective and prone to faking. It is all too easy to project the image you think the interviewer wants. Tests take several forms, the most common of which is perhaps the Rorschach blot test where a candidate is shown ten different ink blots. You have to describe what you see in each one and what thoughts spring to mind.

Studies show that all these tests are somewhat subjective and their accuracy depends very much on the type of person who devises and interprets them. There is no real substitute for the interview as a reliable means of selection, but some firms like to use test results as a back-up. From your point of view, it's probably best to approach them with a sense of humour. Some personnel officers give tests purely to assess applicants' reaction to stress, so rise above it and don't attach too much importance to your results. At the end of the day, it's your achievements and experience which count most.

Your attitude at the interview should be friendly, enthusiastic and professional. Try to project yourself in the best possible light and if you have prepared yourself well, this shouldn't be difficult. Remember that interviews are a two-way process and you should be gleaning as much real information as possible. If you're a top-class candidate, they will be doing a selling job too and it's in your interests to probe through the whitewash.

A favourite approach of personnel officers is to ask how much you know about the company. If you've done your homework well, you can score points here and take the opportunity of asking those questions which sprang to mind as you ploughed through their annual report details. Try to find out:

- if the company is successful and why;
- what their broad objectives and long-term strategy are.

Don't interrogate – you don't want to frighten them off. But do ask sensible, open-ended questions. If the company is doing well, the personnel officer will be only too pleased to tell you about it. If she clams up, then you know there's something wrong somewhere.

Take your lead from the interviewer and answer questions as pleasantly as possible. Nothing puts people off more than a defensive attitude. State your achievements and ambitions positively. Make sure, in a low-key way, that they realise you are someone out of the ordinary.

If you are returning to work, having had a family break, expect questions about child care provisions and have your answers ready. Employers always want to see signs of commitment to a resumed career and they won't be impressed if you haven't thought your home responsibilities through.

Having discussed you, the personnel officer will tell you about the job. Listen attentively and store up any questions until she has finished. Some good things to ask are:

- Why did the present and previous secretaries leave and how long had they been in the post?
- What is the boss really like? Ask for a frank opinion – you may not get one, but no harm in asking.
- Will he give you lots of personal things to do? (This might not be the kind of job you are looking for.)
- Are there any special problems associated with the job? (This can be a tactful way of asking if the boss is a dipsomaniac.)

Try to build up as accurate a picture as possible. When committing yourself for 35 hours a week (at least), you should really try to find out what you're letting yourself in for.

Your next discussion point will be the remuneration package. You should be given details of:

- Salary, and reviews;
- Overtime;
- Method of payment;
- Hours of work;
- Holidays;
- Pension entitlement;
- Sick leave arrangements;
- Information about special perks.

These special perks may include a subsidised mortgage, free lunches, clothing allowance and company car. Make sure you know exactly what is being offered. When it comes down to it, you need to know that this job will keep you in the manner to which you've become accustomed. Should the salary be below par, say so, but don't be tempted to start haggling at this stage. Wait until you've been offered, and want to accept, the job, before ironing out salary problems.

Remuneration aside, you also need to find out how much the company values its secretaries. Do they have ongoing assessments and yearly appraisals? Are there opportunities for further training or advancement? Unless you're applying to a particularly progressive organisation, or to one of the financial institutions, the answer to these questions is likely to be in the negative. However, it does no harm to ask and if enough applicants put the same questions, perhaps employers will feel the need to review their secretarial policies.

You may meet your potential boss there and then, but it's more likely that you will be called back for a second interview if there is competition. Although it's more time-consuming to have two interviews, particularly if you have several irons in the fire, it can help your objectivity. The break between interviews will give you more time to assess the prospects rationally, and you may find your opinion of the job quite different on a separate occasion.

Your second interview is the one that really counts. Meeting your potential boss and deciding if you'll get along is crucial. Working eight hours a day with someone you don't like will be purgatory. During the week you probably spend more waking hours with your boss than your other half, and we all know how careful you were about that choice.

Weighing up someone on a brief meeting is very difficult, particularly if he possesses superficial charm. Try to see through the top layer and look carefully for character guides. Is his office tidy and free from papers? This often shows an orderly mind and someone who likes delegating. Haven't you noticed how the secretive boss, who does everything himself, clings to every scrap of paper?

Is his manner brisk and businesslike? Someone who lingers over his life history won't be the most dynamic person to work for. However, it's just as bad if an interview is dashed through in ten minutes. I was offered a job on the strength of an interview like this, and had to request a second appointment before making up my mind. The potential boss was sufficiently nonplussed when we met again to allow me to put those questions I'd not been able to ask on the first occasion.

What is your boss's style, and is it compatible with yours? Does he sit rigidly behind an executive desk, or do you sit on easy chairs around a coffee table? Does he introduce himself as Mr, or do you know you'll be on first name terms? The most relaxed-looking people have a habit of being petty sticklers for formality.

Does he have a sense of humour (most important), and is it one that appeals to you too? Working for a slapstick prankster can be more tiresome than working for someone with no humour at all. You'll have to weigh up the signs carefully.

What is his attitude to his previous secretary? If you detect anything but warmth, ask some careful questions to find out why. Ask him what he looks for in a secretary. If his eyes lit up when you walked into the room, you will know it's for an ornament. Does he talk down to you, or do you think you'll work in a team? Will he enjoy being organised? Some men positively dote on this, while others will hide in the loo.

What does he hope for in his job? Has he been promoted recently? Is he away from the office much and will you be trusted to run things in his absence? Is he a married nine-to-fiver, or a playboy workaholic with a string of girlfriends to keep unravelled? Will the management of his personal affairs be part of your job (the mechanics rather than the emotions, I hasten to add)?

I'm obviously not suggesting that you ask any of these questions outright. I have touched on some sensitive areas and you'll need to probe around tactfully to get the answers you need. It all helps to build up the picture I keep talking about.

Ask to meet anyone else for whom you'll be working, and with whom you'll share an office. See exactly where you will sit, examine the equipment (not too closely) and make sure you're not relegated to the broom cupboard. This is not as far-fetched as it sounds. In a temp job I was presented with a small trolley which had a typewriter on top, and stationery on the bottom. As the firm was chronically short of accommodation, I had to wheel my trolley around each day looking for an empty office. On bad days, I was installed in the corridor. This little experience taught me the value of decent accommodation.

After the interview, treat yourself to a coffee and write up what's happened while it's fresh in your mind. Try to recall your exact impressions and add to your notes during the day as things come back to you. Look at what you've written the next day and make out an objective list of pros and cons. Try not to be swayed by superficialities – the location may be a dream, but if the boss is a bore, what is the point? Compare your pros and cons with your original criteria and see if they match up. Beware of the 'halo effect' which can make one positive or negative factor cloud the others.

Ask yourself if this job will be a challenge, and an improvement on your present one? Do you think you'll be happy, and will you be able to get along with your new boss and colleagues?

Were you treated courteously at your interview and have subsequent dealings with the company been all they should be? This is extremely important. If potential employees are not treated well, you can imagine how existing staff fare. You should be dealt with graciously and, if not, I hope those warning bells sound.

If you are offered the job, the terms are right and you feel enthusiastic, then you're in with a chance. Never talk yourself into accepting a job which just doesn't feel right. If it doesn't feel right at the interview, it never will. Cut your losses there and then, and begin again. Life is too short to be miserable.

Consider carefully, remember your own worth, and *never* sell yourself short. A challenging job is always around the next corner – it's just a question of finding it.

Now you have the right job, we can turn to the second part of this book which deals with the likely (and unlikely) situations you may come across in your secretarial career. There are times when you'll be asked to produce the impossible and I hope the next section will tell you the things they didn't mention at secretarial college.

# Part 2: The Specifics

# Chapter 3

# Building Up Partnerships

## First days in a new job

Your first few days in a new job will be most important. Your new boss will be looking for the qualities he liked at interview and will want reassurance that he made the right decision in employing you. Your colleagues will be very interested in a newcomer and on the lookout for signs that you'll fit in well. Existing employees tend to be rather critical, and there's nothing they will resent more than a new broom. Despite your curiosity value, try to be as relaxed as possible. Keep your wits about you and make discreet notes on the people you meet. Colleagues will be pleasantly surprised if they don't have to introduce themselves more than once.

It's a popular myth that secretaries spend half their lives having expensive lunches with their bosses, but it *is* possible that he'll take you to lunch on your first day. This will be a valuable opportunity to get to know each other a little better and perhaps reassure you both that you made the right decision too.

Don't be disappointed if you find yourself with only a curled-up sandwich and cup of tea for company, though. Some bosses are distinctly wary of a new secretary and need a little time to get adjusted.

You may be plunged in at the deep end with a great pile of work to do and no one to show you the ropes. Although this might be a bit daunting at first, there is no better way of getting to know a job (unless it happens to be your first, of course). If you are an old hand and have to find things out for yourself, you're more likely to remember them. But if help is offered, accept it gratefully.

If there is time, tidy your desk and go through the filing cabinets. Familiarising yourself with the set-up and knowing exactly where things are will make you feel more at home. Practise using the office equipment. Perhaps there is a computerised telephone system you haven't previously encountered, and the time spent in reading the manual will pay dividends.

If you haven't already been shown round the firm, make a point of introducing yourself to crucial people – the tea lady, post-room clerk, switchboard operator, receptionist, chauffeur and maintenance man.

All these people need to know who and where you are, and for whom you are working. Being on good terms with everyone, but with these very important people in particular, will make your life more agreeable. In an advertising agency I heard of, everyone, including the managing director, made strenuous efforts to keep on the right side of the efficient but somewhat fickle tea lady. There was no one to match her skill at gliding into meetings with aromatic brews – but only if you were in her good books.

Fellow secretaries will be your greatest allies. If sharing an office, make sure you take your turn with the chores from day 1. Be friendly and unobtrusive, letting them know you are happy to be part of the team. Never criticise, even if the office is a shambles. Quietly organise your own corner and hope the others follow suit.

Don't harp on too much about your previous firm. Colleagues are usually interested in your previous experience, but won't like hearing that it was more interesting, or efficient, particularly on the first day. We all draw on past experience but the trick is to keep quiet about it.

Always write down the answers people give to your questions. There is nothing more annoying than being asked the same things over and over again. Talk to your office administrator and make sure you have up-to-date phone lists and office manuals. Being properly genned up can save a lot of unnecessary questions.

If the previous secretary was on the ball, your noticeboard or the wall behind your desk should be a mine of information. If there are only last year's holiday postcards, remove these by degrees and replace them with current data.

## How to cope with your boss

Even the most ardent feminist will know, or soon learn, that it's in her best interests to cosset her boss from the first minute. I am in no way advocating that you become a doormat, or pander to his every whim, but some careful consideration will make life a lot easier for you both. All the most successful secretaries and PAs I know are masters of this approach which in no way detracts from their own individuality.

Much of what has been written about the so-called 'office wife syndrome' is a lot of rubbish as far as my experience goes. There are undoubtedly instances where secretaries, particularly those working for very senior executives, organise the social and personal side of their boss's life (in conjunction with his wife, of course). When you consider that the professional and social lives of many top businessmen are necessarily intertwined, this is not a bit surprising. One of the main functions of the secretary is to save her boss's valuable time and if this includes some personal work (obviously within reason), well, fine. I've been in this position myself and have enjoyed the variety of tasks such involvement brings. (It also provides a good opportunity to get to know your boss's other half.)

However, there are instances when secretaries are abused and this is quite a different matter. Try to avoid such a situation from the start. I heard about a secretary who was asked to buy food for her boss's dog! Even worse was the secretary who had a written request from her boss's wife to buy several tubes of contraceptive jelly. This was a bit much, especially as the chemist had to put through a special order for such a large quantity and gave my friend some very old-fashioned looks from then on!

How can you make an effective stand if put in this difficult position? Speak to your boss calmly and put it to him just how much more work you could handle if freed from his personal errands. Be quiet and reasonable, not giving way to emotion. Reinforce the same message whenever necessary and you will probably have less occasion to do this as time goes on.

At the other end of the spectrum is the secretary who won't give her boss so much as a cup of coffee because this is 'not part of her role'. She's right, of course – it probably isn't. However, I see two reasons for adopting a flexible attitude. First, it's less expensive to the company if you get the coffee rather than your boss whose time probably costs a fortune. Second, a stand on such a trivial point won't help the boss/ secretary relationship you should be trying to establish.

Obviously you have to make up your own mind on all these issues and do what is best for you. However, if you fall within the camp I've just described, make your attitude plain at interviews to save unnecessary aggravation.

Ensure unobtrusively that you're always one step ahead of your boss. After a few months in a new job, you will have demonstrated your initiative (often) and proved that your judgement is sound. It's only when you have shown these skills that your boss will feel he can trust you. If asked a question to which you don't know the answer, always say you'll check and report back. Never bluff your way out of specifics. Your boss will see through you and begin finding things out for himself.

Allow yourself time to fit in with your boss's style. If you overlap with his previous secretary, she will be able to give you some useful tips. If on your own, you'll just have to feel your way in gently. Perhaps he needs a good laugh or screaming rage periodically? Weigh up the signs carefully.

Don't expect too much from your working relationship. There are bound to be times when your boss will retreat into a private world. Don't take this personally – he is probably under strain or pressure. Be understanding and leave him alone. He most likely needs thinking time and won't want to be 'jollied along'.

Above anything else, never betray your boss's trust – it is the most important facet of your relationship. Executives often have difficult times and your boss may confide his worries in you. If asked for an opinion, give it honestly (but tactfully). Otherwise, just listen. Keep any confidences strictly – even from your nearest and dearest, and especially from the office gossip who may try to pump you.

Don't expect constant appreciation, however good a job you do. Most busy executives are under too much pressure to thank their secretaries politely after each completed task (although if the bosses have any sense they'll adopt a generally appreciative manner). However, I'm not suggesting you become a saint and martyr. If taken for granted you'll have to make a stand – and the best of luck to you.

You need to give a new job at least six months before you know it well enough to make a proper judgement. The most important thing is that you get along well with your boss and have the basis of a sound working relationship. If you find you can't stand each other, you may as well cut your losses now – there is absolutely no point in being miserable. But I don't recommend giving up a job lightly. Some good-humoured plain speaking can often restore a relationship which has temporarily gone on the rocks. Never sulk or harbour bad feelings. As I've said before, if you have a genuine grievance tell him about it, as calmly as possible. Don't expect overnight miracles, but cheerfully peg on with your cause.

Even if your boss has sorely tried your patience, don't complain to all and sundry. There is nothing like the office grapevine for exacerbating a minor problem. You may need to let off steam, of course, but far better to confide in one person on whose discretion you can rely than telling all.

Tolerance, patience and adaptability are desirable qualities for all secretaries but particularly so for temps who may encounter a different type of boss each week. What tips are there for coping with a variety of personalities?

- *The workaholic.* Never allow yourself to become ruffled by workaholics (or anyone else for that matter). They can take a perverse delight in rushing others along at their own mad pace. Even in an emergency you will achieve far more by working at a constant rate, and don't let the workaholic convince you otherwise. Take it easy and relax – your frantic boss should appreciate the calming influence.
- *The arrogant type.* Some bosses get away with arrogance because too many people bow and scrape to their lofty position in life. Without

being rude, don't ever pander to this kind of boss – he can make your life a total misery. Be efficient, firm and keep smiling. Most arrogant types have a sense of humour (somewhere) but people are too inhibited by their manner to discover it.

- *The superior type.* There is nothing more frustrating than working for someone who refuses to believe that you have a brain. When you feel the hackles rising, try to keep your sense of humour (even though you might feel like murder). At the same time, prove yourself to be totally efficient and reliable. If the boss has a shred of honesty, his attitude should soften with time. If, however, at the end of a given period, your 'superior' superior is still patronising you, have a discussion with him to find out why. Put across your viewpoint (and capabilities in case these have escaped him) and stress how you could work even better if not treated like a moron.
- *The female boss.* Assuming you are a female secretary then a woman boss should be on your side (after all, we working women have to stick together at times).

A female boss is likely to be more demanding than a male. Any female executive in a position of responsibility has probably had to prove herself many times over, so is likely to be a hard taskmaster. You will probably find yourself working very hard but should be rewarded by a more understanding attitude when you're feeling below par.

## Sexual harassment

There is ample evidence from recent studies that sexual harassment is a widespread problem throughout the international workplace.

In May 1990 the Council of Ministers of the European Community (EC) adopted a resolution on 'The Dignity of Men and Women at Work' which defines sexual harassment as any 'unwanted conduct of a sexual nature or other conduct based on sex affecting the dignity of women and men at work'. Sexual harassment is behaviour that is 'unwanted, unreasonable and offensive to the recipient'. It is wrong to use 'a person's rejection of . . . such conduct . . . as a basis for a decision which affects that person's employment'. The resolution adds that sexual harassment arises when 'such conduct creates an intimidating, hostile or humiliating work environment for the recipient'. Sexual harassment does not have to be 'sexual' in the sense of being an attempt to initiate sexual relations. It is sufficient that a man or woman is singled out because of their gender. Anyone who is victimised because of a complaint of sexual harassment is seen to be suffering from further harassment.

Different people have varying tolerance levels of behaviour which could be construed as harassment. Some take exception to the odd risqué joke, while others see nothing wrong and join in. To complicate matters further, there is often a certain amount of informal bantering between the sexes at work. This can be amusing and a bit of innocent light relief. A problem arises when it goes too far or is unreciprocated. Matters can deteriorate further when unwanted physical attentions are sought.

In my teens I worked for a man who could not conduct a conversation without trying to put his arm around me first. I went to extreme lengths to avoid this revolting behaviour – largely by ensuring that there was a desk (at least) between us at all times. Unfortunately, I did not have the emotional maturity to be able to make a formal complaint and deal with the matter properly. I just hoped the problem would go away. When it didn't I saw no alternative but to get another job – this is an all-too-frequent end result of sexual harassment.

### How frequently does the problem occur?

Recent surveys have indicated that sexual harassment is widespread and that the victims are overwhelmingly female. A large-scale study in West Germany found 200,000 women had left their jobs as a result of sexual harassment. A similar survey in Greece discovered that 40 per cent of women experienced sexual harassment during their working lives. A survey by the UK Labour Research Department in 1987 found that 73 per cent of employees reported some form of harassment, 45 per cent of them complaining of superiors harassing subordinates. The most common types of harassment reported overall were 'suggestive remarks or other verbal abuse' (48 per cent), 'sexist or patronising behaviour' (45 per cent) and 'unnecessary touching/unwanted contact' (34 per cent). Other surveys carried out by NALGO, various teaching unions, the Alfred Marks Bureau and the NUS support these findings.

Bosses and colleagues are not always the perpetrators of sexual harassment. The *Guardian* (22 September 1990) reported a case where a senior secretary, responsible for screening her boss's visitors, was harassed by a regular visitor. He took to showing her pornographic magazines with pictures of women who were, like her, of oriental appearance, in explicit clothing and sexual positions. He suggested she would look good like that too. He always made sure there were no witnesses. She dreaded having to deal with him and contemplated asking for a transfer. Fortunately she sought help, though it took months of counselling to overcome her embarrassment, anger and self-blame. She eventually summoned the courage to tell the man clearly that his behaviour was unacceptable and reported the incidents to her boss.

### Why does sexual harassment occur?

Sexual harassment is still widely seen by men as a joke and until recently it was not regarded as a serious problem. A common male response is: 'I wish a woman would sexually harass me.' Sexual harassment often has nothing to do with 'lust' and is commonly an exhibition of power. The National Council for Civil Liberties (NCCL) suggests that a certain type of man needs to reassert in the workplace what he views as his traditional male dominance. The fact that there are now more female executives could perhaps exacerbate this situation. However, some surveys have indicated that sexual harassment is less likely to occur when there are roughly equal numbers of men and women working together and they have similar status.

## Just how far does harassing behaviour go?
Sexual harassment is not about trivial incidents but about systematic, repeated and unwanted sexual advances, physical or verbal, which threaten and humiliate, undermine job performance, perhaps blocking promotion or training opportunities. Secretaries have even been threatened with dismissal for refusing to make love with their bosses.

Doris Hawley of the Banking, Insurance and Finance Union is one of a network of counsellors in the UK which provides support and advice to victims of sexual harassment. She says that no woman she has ever talked to has ever complained after only one or two incidents. Sadly, and often to their detriment, they give the man the benefit of the doubt – and he just continues.

## Action you can take
We can therefore see that sexual harassment is a real problem and a complex one to solve. Wht steps should you take if you find yourself a victim? First, find out if your company has a complaints procedure for dealing with sexual harassment. Since the first successful legal action against sexual harassment in 1986 many organisations have begun to take sexual harassment seriously and have instituted their own complaints, counselling and disciplinary action procedures. The European Commission's Code of Conduct, expected to be drawn up by July 1991, will, it is to be hoped, spur more to do the same.

The NCCL, who are preparing an updated booklet on sexual harassment in 1991, suggest the following course of action:

1. Talk to other women in the workplace. Find out if the harasser has behaved this way towards others. You will gain support and self-confidence from discovering that you are not alone.
2. Get together with other women and talk about what to do. Try to form a women's group. If you work in a large organisation you could use a questionnaire to get more information about the experience of other women and their views. You can give the

43

   results to your union representative (if your workplace is unionised) and/or to management when discussing further action.
3. Collect evidence of the harassment. Write down what is done, or said, and when.
4. Ask the harasser to stop behaving in this way – by letter if you wish. If you can, ask a friend or colleague to be with you when you confront him. Be specific about what offends you. Many men are not conscious of the fact that jokes, and touching in particular, are offensive.
5. You might find it useful to return like with like, to show men what harassment feels like – for instance, pinning up pictures of naked men or whistling and grabbing at men. Some women do not want to use this tactic.
6. Speak to your shop steward if you have one. If this is not possible – for instance, if he is the harasser – go to your district official.
7. Suggest to management that it is in their interests to have a procedure that deals with sexual harassment to improve working conditions.

If these steps do not work, you could take your case to court. Although the words 'sexual harassment' do not occur in the Sex Discrimination Act 1975, the Act does state that it is unlawful for an employer to discriminate against a woman employed by him 'by dismissing her, or subjecting her to any other detriment'. Case law has established that sexual harassment amounts to 'any other detriment'. In order to be detrimental treatment, the conduct must have been unwelcome to the recipient and must be sufficiently severe to affect working conditions. Isolated trivial incidents are unlikely to be sufficient. However, the more serious the level of harassment the less need there is to show more than an isolated incident.

The principal remedy for sexual harassment under the Sex Discrimination Act is damages. Employees are entitled to compensation for loss of earnings if they are dismissed as a result of resisting sexual advances and to damages for injury to feelings. It is usually necessary to obtain medical evidence to confirm the harm which has been done to the employee's general wellbeing, which will often cover depression, sleeplessness and deterioration in personal relationships resulting from the feeling of humiliation which the employee will have suffered. It is also possible to claim constructive dismissal if a woman feels forced to resign because of the severity of the harassment.

Recourse to an industrial tribunal may be more successful. According to the Equal Opportunities Commission there have been 85 substantive industrial tribunal decisions on sexual harassment complaints. Of these,

44 applications were successful. The average compensation awarded to successful sexual harassment complainants is comparatively high. Among the employers recently found liable for sexual harassment are Bracebridge Engineering (£3050 compensation awarded), Cahill Motor Engineering (£1000), Greenwich Health Authority (£6235), Fenton Barns (£3731), Smith Anderson and Co (£1000), Kebbles Restaurant (£2250) and Gateway Foodmarkets (£7000, £1000 and £750 to three applicants following lesbian harassment). Out of court settlements may be even higher. The London Borough of Islington, for example, recently paid £15,000 in an out-of-court settlement to a former employee because of sexual harassment. A number of claims have also been brought in the ordinary courts for breach of contract, for assault and false imprisonment. All the cases brought in the ordinary courts so far (1991) have been settled before going to trial.

Bringing a claim can, however, be something of an ordeal and women have been questioned on their attitudes to sexual matters, their manner and their dress. The Employment Appeal Tribunal, for example, has stated that whether a woman was 'provocative' in manner and dress at work is a relevant factor in determining the degree of discrimination and detriment suffered by her when amounts of compensation were determined. In a case in 1988 (*Wileman* v *Minilec Engineering Ltd*) Ms Wileman was awarded the meagre sum of £50 after four and a half years of (proven) physical and verbal harassment. You may consider that the compensation payments do not merit the effort and distress a court case would cause. As a matter of principle, however, the more court cases there are, the more harassers will be deterred.

This is, therefore, a difficult problem and one which often leaves victims feeling that they were in some way to blame. It is important to dress professionally and bear in mind that, as well as looking the part for work, you have to act the part too. Have a laugh and joke when appropriate and keep a sense of humour (what secretary can do without it?), but always draw a fine line between yourself and male colleagues who may misinterpret your innocent fun.

Now that positive action is being taken against it, let us all hope that sexual harassment is less of a problem in the future. The experts I have consulted are agreed, however, that if you should find yourself a victim, the worst thing you can do is to leave the job without resolving matters. Your career record will suffer and the problem will remain for another innocent victim.

For further advice contact:

Equal Opportunities Commission, Overseas House, Quay Street, Manchester M3 3HN; tel 061-833 9244; fax 061-835 1657. The EOC can provide advice and information on all aspects of sexual harassment at work and will, where circumstances warrant it, take up a case on your behalf.

National Council for Civil Liberties (Liberty), 21 Tabard Street, London SE1 4LA; tel 071-403 3888; fax 071-407 5354. The NCCL no longer provides advice to the general public but will advise 'advice givers'.

Women Against Sexual Harassment, 242 Pentonville Road, London N1 9UN; tel 071-833 0222. In addition to advising you, they can provide a booklet for your employer entitled *Introducing a Sexual Harassment Policy in the Workplace: An Employer's Guide*.

For a full review of the legal principles and case law relating to sexual harassment get a copy of *Preventing and Remedying Sexual Harassment at Work: A Resource Manual* by M. Rubenstein, available from Industrial Relations Services, 18–20 Highbury Place, London N5 1QP.

# Chapter 4

# The Mechanics

You have no chance of developing a secretarial role until you've mastered the mechanics. How can you be expected to organise your boss if you can't organise yourself?

You therefore have to prove yourself in your own domain when starting a new job (and particularly if you're not very experienced). Establish systems and procedures; and make sure that your own office runs like clockwork. It is only then that you will be able to expand your proven efficiency into other areas and fully develop your role. Your boss will feel confident in your growing abilities and you will begin to work as a real team. It's a goal well worth working towards.

## Using your time productively

You need to give a job your very best without becoming its slave. Not everyone shares my view, but there is no better start to the working day than getting to the office early. This enables you to sort out priorities and get organised in the peaceful lull before your boss arrives and the switchboard opens.

You obviously need to be flexible about working hours, particularly when there's a panic, but as a general rule, make sure you go home on time. Take a proper lunch hour, away from the office. A sandwich lunch at your desk is all very well but it won't feel as though you've had a proper break. It's difficult to maintain high standards when working long hours for a prolonged period. Mistakes are bound to occur. Emergencies apart, you should be able to cope with your job in the allotted time – if not, look for an assistant.

Of course, there are exceptions. The small proportion of very senior PAs who work for the UK's top executives probably don't have a minute to themselves and have to be completely committed to their careers. But they really are in a class of their own.

While I cannot over-emphasise the importance of good working relationships, try not to spend too much time gossiping (however tempting this may be). If you're under pressure every minute is precious. However, never cut back on courtesy and pleasantries. They are as essential as the air we breathe. Here are some tips on using your time productively:

- Organise priorities and do essentials first thing in the morning (no matter how boring they may be). You'll enjoy that feeling of self-congratulation for the rest of the day.
- Be methodical and don't flit from one task to another. This, of course, contradicts the role of the secretary which is essentially one of coping with a hundred things all at once. However, try to keep an orderly mind and work in some kind of logical sequence.
- Be tidy and keep things neat, unless you're happiest working in a muddle (like the university lecturer who kept all his papers stacked on the chairs lining his office. Meetings were conducted standing up, but he could find even the smallest scrap of paper in an instant).
- Make sure that your office equipment is in tip-top condition and that you carry plentiful supplies of those items used regularly.
- Try to be brief. Never waste time initiating correspondence when a phone call will do. Use compliments slips instead of covering memos when sending material to colleagues.
- Assuming you have an assistant or a willing colleague, don't be afraid to delegate. You will have to accept that delegated tasks might not be handled in your own way but it's far better that work is handled adequately to time rather than being left for ever pending. However, keep a close eye on progress – you will always retain responsibility for any delegated end product.

## All about lists

There is nothing better for improving efficiency than drawing up a daily list. When you have a hundred and one things to accomplish, listing helps to assess their priority and should stem any feelings of panic. With your daily tasks written down, you won't feel nearly so awe-inspired by the amount you have to do.

Try to keep two lists – one routine and one urgent. Check through the diary and bring-forward system each morning (or the night before) and note down what has to be done. Making a habit of this daily check should ensure that nothing slips through the net, particularly when the pressure's really on.

You will have to decide which kind of list suits you best. Some secretaries use ordinary lined pads. Others use cards – these will save time in writing a completely new list every day as you can carry forward tasks. The card is then destroyed once the matter has been dealt with.

The crucial thing about lists is actioning them – if you don't, stop wasting your time. You are obviously not a list person. By the same token, if you find yourself noting down tasks day after day, they can get relegated to extremely low priority or forgotten altogether. They couldn't have been very important.

## Diaries

You will find it easier to organise your boss's time if you maintain one large diary only. It is asking for trouble and endless confusion if you and your boss maintain individual diaries into which you both book appointments. You will waste time updating and cross-referencing or, if you are too busy to do this, will find your boss is double booked and/or missing meetings. If there are particular reasons why your boss needs a duplicate diary, be meticulous in noting down any appointments made.

If you have any say in the matter, try to ensure that:

- You hold the one office diary;
- All appointment requests come to you;
- All diary entries are made in pencil (nothing is ever certain).

If your boss needs to make a further appointment when he is out at a meeting, he can simply tell the other party that their secretaries should liaise. It is a waste of valuable executive time if he starts jiggling appointments.

As well as recording business engagements, the diary should be the master book into which you can note all crucial birthdays, anniversaries, car service dates, health appointments etc. If your boss has to attend evening engagements or is making overnight trips, it's a good idea to photocopy the relevant diary pages for his wife. She will appreciate knowing his movements if he's forgotten to mention them. When making evening arrangements it is also courteous to check with her first to avoid any double booking. More about the mechanics of booking appointments in Chapter 5.

## Addresses

The golden rule here is to keep a full record of the name, title, address, telephone number and fax number of anyone with whom you come into business contact – however casual the contact may seem. You never know when you may need to track the person down again.

There are many different address recording systems – books, card indexes etc – and your prime requirement in selecting these should be ease of update and overall clarity. A typed card index is easy to read, quick to flip through (with one hand) and simple to update.

A book is perhaps more compact but handwritten entries will look extremely messy once they've been updated a few times. If this system is your preference, you could type each entry on an adhesive label before placing it in the appropriate place. At least there will be no strange squiggles to decipher. This system can be used if your boss needs an abbreviated address record for carrying around.

Kardex are one of the best-known filing and storage system manufacturers, and you can obtain details of all their range from: Kardex Systems (UK) Ltd, UK Sales Headquarters, High Cross Centre, Fountayne Road, London N15 4TX; tel 081-885 5588.

## Handling the post

Try to open your post as soon as possible – you never know what crucial information it may contain. If you feel benevolent save the postage stamps – many charities get much-needed cash for them (eg British Kidney Patient Association, Bordon, Hants GU35 9JP).

You need to agree with your boss exactly what you can open. As a general rule, I have always opened anything marked 'confidential' but not 'personal'. Pay slips are obviously sacrosanct. If you open something sensitive which was incorrectly marked, give the letter and envelope to your boss with a brief apology.

Read each letter carefully and link up with any previous correspondence. Make sure that your boss has all the information he'll need in order to reply. This might involve you in making a few phone calls. So as not to delay things, you could pass the letter through with a note to your boss saying that you are pursuing any queries. If you are in a position to deal with the complete letter for your boss, jot a note to keep him informed. It might be that there were subtleties you could not appreciate. Alternatively you could draft a complete reply for his signature.

As far as outgoing post is concerned, there are a few golden rules on the mechanics:

- Keep an eye on your boss's grammar. Unless he is hyper-sensitive (or a lawyer) he'll probably appreciate a bit of judicious text correction.
- Check your spelling carefully and keep a dictionary close by. When in doubt, look it up.
- Proof-read everything you type, no matter how rushed you might be. A busy executive won't be impressed by typing errors.
- Never use correcting fluid on a letter – nothing looks more unprofessional.

## Dictation and transcription

Always concentrate when taking dictation. This might sound silly, but it's surprising how automatically you can take down shorthand, your thoughts completely elsewhere. This is fine if your shorthand is faultless. However, if you are at all like me, any lapses in concentration can make the reading back well nigh impossible.

Coping with a difficult dictator can require some strength of character. You're bound to encounter the boss who mumbles in the opposite direction; or dictates at high speed; or perhaps both. I once temped for a man like this and attributing his pronounced slur to a stroke, struggled with his high-speed dictation for more than an hour. When left with pages of unreadable shorthand, I regretted that I hadn't queried sentences or told him to slow down (especially when I found his speech impediment was due to drink). If in doubt, ask.

As soon as you've taken dictation, read your shorthand through. If there are more than a couple of words you can't read, type a double-spaced draft and take it to your boss, cap in hand. I guarantee he'll fill in the blanks without complaint, and will probably change the text anyway.

Type up your shorthand as soon as possible and try not to leave it overnight. It has been my sad experience that the longer shorthand is left, the less memory will aid transcription of those hieroglyphics.

If you're not a shorthand buff, I can recommend the dictaphone. You run the risk of high-speed mumblers with this method too, but at least you can replay the tape to your heart's content (and enlist the help of your colleagues). When under pressure, the dictaphone can save the time you'd normally spend closeted with your boss taking dictation. Unfortunately, this can encourage your boss to use the machine just about anywhere and you'll get some interesting background noises as a result (opera, running bath water, feet pattering to the station – to name but a few).

The latest dictaphones have made great advances and overcome many previous drawbacks. Tapes can show the number of dictated items with their length (most important in deciding what size paper to use), and can give particular instructions or afterthoughts with a special key. Of course, you can adjust the speed of playback and voice tone as always. What more could you ask for?

## Filing and information systems

Mention the word 'filing' to any secretary and there will probably be a loud groan. It is ironic that filing is one of those crucial but boring activities which can too easily be left on one side while more urgent matters are dealt with. You are then in the paradoxical situation of taking more time searching for unfiled papers than if you'd made time to file them in the first place. What can be done to alleviate this remarkably common problem?

Unless you inherit a first-class filing system, devise one which suits you. Having gone to this amount of trouble you will be strongly motivated to keep it in order. There are all kinds of filing systems and you will know which one appeals to you. Try to keep it simple – a treble cross-referenced system may look impressive, but if it takes 20 minutes to track down a memo, what is the point?

Keep your typed filing list in a prominent place so that others (even your boss) will be able to find things if you're away from the office. Tracer cards are an essential part of a booking-out system, if a number of people have access to your files. Confidential items should be kept in a safe, or in your boss's office.

If it's totally impossible for you to do the filing every day (and who can?), keep an expanding sectioned file nearby into which you can sort your papers as they are dealt with. This saves wading through great mounds of paper awaiting filing if you need something in a hurry – it also speeds up the filing process once you're able to get down to it.

As well as keeping documents tidily, filing gives a valuable opportunity to check on their current status. Nothing should be filed until the subject matter is closed – unless you are involved in some long-running saga, of course. Read through each piece of filing and ask yourself if the points raised have been fully dealt with. If not, the matter can be resurrected and appropriate action taken. Making this final check is a most worthwhile task. Unless you or your boss have the memory of an elephant, it is virtually impossible to remember everything. This little exercise will help to keep you both on the ball.

It goes without saying that only relevant information should be stored away in your files. If you're new to the job, deciding on relevant information may be difficult initially, and you will have to tread carefully. A friend of mine worked for someone who obligingly put a green line through anything which could be filed in the wastepaper basket. This saved both of them wading through trivia and left only one person to blame if important papers were destroyed. Not all bosses take this trouble, however, and it's usually secretaries who make these executive decisions in the end. When in doubt, file it.

If your office has new technology you may be able to banish conventional filing for ever. It is a simple matter to have your processor 'file' away information on to disk. If your boss needs papers for a meeting, it is easy to print out those required. Confidential papers can be kept away from prying eyes more effectively on special disks with security codes. Space can be saved with cabinet-free offices. The system obviously has many benefits, although a junior secretary may have to be responsible for inputting incoming mail on the disk files.

As an alternative, you may choose to have your files micro-filmed. This is a very cost-effective form of bulk data storage and comes into its own when exact replicas of documents, such as invoices and drawings, are required. How does the system work?

Photographs are taken of the storage information which is reproduced on to either:

- *Roll film* – where documents are stored sequentially, like cine film;
- *Microfiche* – where documents are stored in rows on picture postcard-sized film; or
- *Jacket* – where documents are filed on roll film which is cut into strips and stored in transparent jackets. (This medium lends itself to situations where updating information is required.)

Irrespective of the storage method, a 'reading' machine is used when information needs to be traced. You may have come across these machines in your local library. Some readers have a photocopying facility which can produce hard paper copies, and some are linked to a computer-aided retrieval system. For further information about micro-film you can obtain a free booklet from: Bell & Howell Ltd, 33–35 Woodthorpe Road, Ashford, Middlesex TW15 2RZ; tel 0784 251234; telex 266119; fax 0784 259286.

Depending on the business you are in, you may have to set up an information system. If your boss writes regular reports on a given subject, it might be an idea to scour newspapers, magazines etc for relevant file clippings. When he finds that you have current information to hand, he should be sufficiently impressed to give you a pay rise on the spot!

## Bring forward systems

An efficient 'bring forward' system is a must for the busy secretary. Make a point of keeping on one side the file copy of anything which leaves your office requiring an answer (make a photocopy if it's something that you haven't actually typed). Pencil on the date a few days hence when you should start chasing a reply. Store the papers in an expanding file numbered 1 to 31 under the appropriate date, and you are all set. Other information, including correspondence about lunch appointments, meeting notes, invitations etc can be stored in this way too and the only thing left to chance will be remembering to check the file each morning.

As well as enabling you to keep tabs on all your paperwork, the correspondence process in general should be hastened. Recipients will soon realise what happens if they don't reply promptly. You will get a reputation for amazing efficiency and your boss will be reassured to know that even if his memory is unreliable, there is an infallible back-up system.

## The day file

A meticulously kept day file is worth its weight in gold. Take an extra copy of anything you type (preferably on different coloured paper from the file copy) and store it chronologically in a central file. If ever you misplace the filing, or need to check a letter reference in double quick time, your day file will always turn up trumps. We are none of us 100 per cent reliable, and it's always as well to have your own text back-up system. Of course, if you have a word processor, you can simply check on your disk, and no problem.

If you receive a lot of telexes and/or facsimiles, you can keep a day file of these too. There are always several copies of each and it is easy to keep a spare in the same chronological file described above. However, faxes deteriorate rapidly with time and will be illegible within a year. If you receive essential information by fax, either take a photocopy for storage or deal with the matter quickly! (Some of the very latest fax machines use 'plain' rather than 'coated' paper and this should have a normal lifespan in storage.)

## Producing reports

There can be nothing more daunting than having to transform a large wad of illegible writing into a professional-looking report. You may have very little warning of this herculean task, and even less time in which to complete it. Having said that, however, it is surprising what can be achieved in a short space of time if you know a few tricks of the trade.

If you have access to a word processor, or better still desktop publishing software and a laser printer, report production is far easier. Unfortunately, some companies still do not have these facilities so it is worth mentioning traditional systems.

### Layout
Discuss the report presentation with your boss. Ascertain the precise page location of:

- Left- and right-hand margins;
- Page start and end;

- Page numbering (usually top right-hand corner or centre bottom);
- First heading.

With this format information you can draw a backing sheet to be used behind every sheet of typed paper. This will ensure a standard layout, which is particularly important if there are several typists. A sample backing sheet is shown on page 55.

Before typing a single word, you also need to check the following:

- Paragraph indentation;
- Numbering style for figures and/or graphs;
- Style of main and subheadings (and if underlined);
- Line spacing (most important);
- Use of 'bullets' (these little black blobs I'm so fond of – achieved by filling in a typewritten nought with black felt tip).

If there are several typists, it's a good idea to type out the decisions about layout so everyone knows what they're doing.

If there are several authors, check through the complete report for continuity of style – particularly with paragraphs, sub-paragraphs etc. If someone has time to do a proper editing job, so much the better.

## Supplies

Decide how your report is to be presented and bound, and ensure that you have adequate stocks of the items you'll need – spiral binders, covers etc. There's nothing more frustrating at the end of a hectic period to find the report cannot be finalised because stocks are short. If using graphs, check that you have sufficient acetate and slide carriers.

## Graphics

Look through the report to see if there are any graphs or diagrams to be prepared. These can be handled by:

- Your in-house graphics specialist (pure luxury);
- An outside graphics artist (for one-off jobs);
- You.

Graphics specialists are accustomed to tight deadlines, but it is only fair to give them as much notice as possible, so get your graphs under way. Take a photocopy of the graphic rough before you do so and keep this in its correct place in the handwritten master version. At least you'll then have a reminder of which graph goes where when the pressure hots up.

The reprographics/printing unit of many colleges, polytechnics and universities take on external work on a commercial basis and they will have the technology to produce excellent graphics (or even the whole report if it is an especially important one).

**Sample backing sheet**

page numbering ____

main heading

start of text

end of text

____

page numbering

If you cannot track down a graphics specialist (or there isn't time) you may have to turn artist yourself. Do not despair – it is amazing what can be achieved with some magic lettering (Letraset etc). Consult your local art shop manager and go through the lettering catalogues. As well as the letters you'd expect (in an infinite variety of styles and sizes), there is a big selection of numbers, symbols, borders and illustrations. So if you're not a natural artist – relax. Straight lines come out well if drawn with a fine black felt tip pen. Try to use a clear plastic ruler – it's easier to see what you're doing.

Some of the graphs and diagrams may form the basis of slides for a formal presentation. If you have a heat transferring machine or special photocopier, the paper graph can be transposed on to acetate sheets. These are Sellotaped into cardboard slide carriers and hey presto! For more sophisticated results, a graphics specialist can draw the diagram directly on to acetate. This is not a job I'd recommend unless you have clear, artistic writing and an exceptionally steady hand.

Of course, if you have a micro-processor with graphics software you can achieve impressive diagrams at the touch of a button.

### The rough draft

Now you can begin typing. If you use a standard typewriter this particular stage will be one hard slog. Unless your boss is expecting a major re-write, type the draft in exactly the same format as the final version. You might then be lucky enough to salvage some draft pages if the correcting pen has not been too vigorous. Page number the typed sheets on the reverse in pencil as you go along. The numbering can then be shuffled around at the correction stage, but you won't be in total confusion if the whole lot gets dropped in the process.

When the draft is typed, make a photocopy for your boss's alterations. This will save rubbing out pencil corrections on the master.

### The final version

When you get the corrected draft, check through it quickly and assess the damage. Straightforward alterations can be changed with correcting fluid which won't show on your final photocopy. If the paragraph order has been changed but little else, you can cut and paste. Snip around unaltered sections and stick these on to fresh sheets of paper using clear Sellotape (Magitape etc) or, for the best results, spray-on glue (eg Spray Mount). Take a photocopy, paint out the paragraph edge lines and copy again. It may, of course, be quicker to do a straight retype.

When typing the final report there are two golden rules:

- Page number on the reverse in pencil; and

- Keep all the rough draft reject pages on one side in case they're reinstated.

If you have some large charts to type which won't fit on to the actual paper size you'll have to be a bit devious. Type them using A3 paper and a long carriage machine, spacing them centrally. Reduce them down to your chosen paper size on the photocopier and you're all set.

When the final text has been approved, slot in the paper graphs and diagrams, together with any reduced typed charts. Number the graphs, diagrams and charts using the format decided. This is usually in accordance with their text chapter, eg charts appearing in Chapter 3 will be Figures 3.1, 3.2, 3.3 etc and should be noted separately from the pagination – perhaps directly underneath.

Page number the whole report and do the contents page. Try to get someone to check this and proof-read with you (but not the boss or he might make more changes). Once the report is perfect, you can go on to photocopy and bind. File the typed original carefully – you never know when you might need more copies or an update.

If you need special photocopying services, such as special reductions or colour, and do not have access to a suitable machine, there are excellent copyshops which are listed in your Yellow Pages under Copying and Duplicating.

## Telephones and telecommunications

The telephone is both a boon and a nuisance. We all appreciate the benefits of telephone communications without which the business world would collapse. Services are improving rapidly and these days all sorts of things are possible, eg video conferencing.

However, the telephone can be a great time-waster. It is possible to spend frustrating hours tracking down callers, and then missing return calls. There are the interruptions too which the telephone brings, often from callers whose queries could be settled by someone else.

But this is where the effective secretary comes in – ensuring that her boss sees only the positive side of the telephone by shielding him from the negative. How is this achieved?

It goes without saying that you should always be totally helpful on the telephone (even when there's a panic on). You know yourself how frustrating it is to call someone whose secretary just can't be bothered. When people ring, get their full details – name, title, company, phone and fax numbers – checking spelling if necessary. Unless it's a 'regular', ask about the nature of the call and if you can help. You can then judge whether to:

- Handle the query yourself;
- Re-route the call if this is appropriate;
- Put the call through to your boss.

If working for a senior executive, be on your guard against cagey 'personal callers' who are often insurance reps. With experience you can develop an instinct for them and deal with the calls accordingly. However, this should not prejudice you against genuine personal callers who will not appreciate an interrogation. You will have to tread carefully.

Develop good relationships with your callers – especially the regulars and other secretaries. This fosters a spirit of mutual co-operation – always important.

The telephone can bring out the worst in people at times as any telephonist will tell you. Try not to lose your temper with a caller who's rude or abrupt. A slanging match won't get you anywhere.

Get all your boss's calls. There can be no greater waste of executive time than dialling phone numbers. If you have a string of calls to make and the first party isn't available, it's probably best to ring again at the end rather than request a return call when you know the phone will be engaged.

You will need an effective message system for the times when your boss in unavailable. It should try to ensure that messages reach him as soon as he's free, whether you are at your desk or not. There are a number of different systems:

- *Verbal messages.* These work well if you are around. You get instant feedback and action can be taken then and there. The system fails completely if you happen to be in the loo at the crucial moment.
- *Written (or typed) messages.* This system is more reliable than verbal messages if you're out of the office, provided you can rely upon your boss to check in some pre-arranged message spot, eg his 'in' tray on your desk.

   Some people find that a message book is both difficult to ignore and a useful record of telephone calls. A line through each message will signify when it's been received. Attach a pencil to the book for this purpose.

   Individual notes (preferably typed) on separate slips of paper are flimsy but flexible. If the message is straightforward it can be ticked and returned to you to show receipt. If further action is needed, the slip of paper will serve as a reminder of this – be it a return call or something more complex.

There may also be times when it's imperative that you contact your boss while he's out of the office. If he has a fixed schedule and you know where you can call him, fine. Otherwise a pocket radiophone or pager is invaluable.

- *Paging systems*. Many executives now have a 'pager' – a portable pocket-sized device that 'beeps' or vibrates when you call him. British Telecom pagers cover most of the UK and offer several different communications options. Gone are the days when pagers simply beeped! Now you can relay telephone numbers for him to call, remind him about appointment times and even send short messages which appear on the pager's small screen.

  With the advent of the European Single Market many executives will be spending more time abroad. If your boss has occasional trips to Europe you can hire a Euromessage pager from BT which will allow you to reach him instantly in major towns, cities and industrial areas in France, Germany and Italy (you don't even have to know which country he's in). And if he strays outside the coverage zone for any length of time he can ring a special message check number and have any messages retransmitted to him. For more information about British Telecom paging call 0800 616111 (freefone).

- *Mobile telephone systems* are increasingly popular with representatives, consultants and other executives who necessarily spend a lot of time 'in the field'. They also make life a lot easier if you need to speak to your boss while he's out. Don't call him for trivial reasons – he may be engaged in important discussions. Save anything but the most urgent queries and messages for when he gets back or calls in.

## British Telecom

British Telecom (BT) is such a vast organisation that it is impossible here to do justice to the range of services available.

### International services

BT produces a free booklet called *Phoning Abroad: The Business Handbook* which gives a good résumé of international services. The guide provides international, country and area codes worldwide, together with charge bands, ringing/engaged tones and time differences (relative to GMT).

- International dialling direct (IDD) allows you to dial direct from almost any UK phone to 600 million phones in over 195 countries.
- Translation services are available for phoning, faxing and telexing abroad. The British Telecom Translation Bureau can provide a

professional multilingual team who offer text translations, on-line telephone interpreting, interpreters for meetings and conferences, and who will even make business calls on your behalf (eg market research, hotel/travel reservations) and report back to you. For more information contact BT's Translation Bureau on 071-492 7222.

- Two useful leaflets are 'International Homecall', showing easy ways to phone the UK from abroad, and 'Home Country Direct Card', a card to help your foreign visitors with little English make calls to their home country using the Home Country Direct Service.

- There are facilities for calling your boss if he's on a ship or airliner.

    For ships call 0800 378 389 and ask for the Ship's Telephone Service. If the ship has satellite communications, dial 155 and ask the international operator for an Inmarsat call. If the ship has satellite communications and you are calling from an exchange with digital technology, you can dial direct by using the appropriate ocean region code:

| | |
|---|---|
| Atlantic Ocean East | 871 |
| Atlantic Ocean West | 874 |
| Pacific Ocean | 872 |
| Indian Ocean | 873 |

and the ship's identification number. International Directory Enquiries on 153 can provide you with ship's identification numbers. To find out if you can dial direct, call BT Inmarsat on 071-492 4996.

For airliners you can call BT's Skyphone Service. For information about Skyphone phone 0800 899 998.

- BT's MultiMessaging Service is geared to sending attractively presented sales messages or information to a number of contacts abroad via fax or telex. For information phone 071-492 7444.

- International conference calls (for 3–60 people) are also possible and may save a lot of time and expense in bringing people together for an international conference. UK conference calls can also be arranged. For further information phone 0800 282 429.

For a copy of *Phoning Abroad: The Business Handbook* contact BT Communications Centre, Business Handbook, Freepost (BS6832), Burnham-on-Sea, Somerset TA9 3BR; tel 0800 272 172.


*National services*
BT do not issue a general booklet on national services but do produce a

quarterly booklet called *In Touch* which outlines the latest products and services available. They also produce a quarterly newsletter *Business News* specifically for business users. To order *In Touch* and/or *Business News* phone 0800 800 806.

Some UK services worth noting are:

- *Prestel*. This is BT's public videotex service which links adapted computers (and TV sets) via ordinary telephone lines providing information and two-way services. Information is selected using the keyboard (or keypad) and displayed on the screen. A vast amount of information is available including news, weather, entertainment, noticeboards and travel timetables. Two-way services allow users to 'talk back' to the computer – to order goods (teleshopping), book tickets, request brochures, pay bills. A 'mailbox' service enables users to communicate with each other by sending/receiving 'message pages'. There is also a link to the telex service. For more information contact: Prestel Sales Office, British Telecom, Network House, Brindley Way, Apsley, Hemel Hempstead, Herts HP3 9RR; tel 0800 200 700.
- *Telecom Gold*. BT's Business Communications Service provides a simple, fast and economical way of sending word processed information, computing files and spreadsheets from one computer to another (see Electronic mail in Chapter 9). Telecom Gold also provides links to BT's radiopaging service. For more information contact Telecom Gold on 0800 200 700 or write to Network House at the address above.
- *Electronic Yellow Pages (EYP)*. EYP is a database of information on 1.8 million businesses and services throughout the UK. The EYP service is available 24 hours a day throughout the year and is accessible via a personal computer with a modem. The system is easy to use: you are asked to key in a location (eg Cardiff or London) plus one other piece of information (eg the name of a business or a type of service) in order to search for a particular company or service. For a user guide and further information contact Electronic Yellow Pages, Yellow Pages, Queens Walk, Reading RG1 7PT; tel 0734 506506.
- *Talking Pages*. This is a telephone information service available in the West Midlands, Avon and Sussex. Trained operators help callers to find information on businesses, services and entertainments in the UK. Information available includes opening hours, credit card acceptance and whether there are facilities for disabled people. The service is available seven days a week from 8 am–12 pm and is charged at normal call rates. Talking pages is available

on: 0273 542222 (Sussex area); 0272 299992 (Avon area); and 021-711 1177 (West Midlands area).

## Mercury Communications

Mercury Communications is part of the Cable and Wireless Group and was licensed to compete with BT in 1982. While still a relative newcomer when set against BT's long-standing and well-established market, Mercury has put forward an ambitious programme in order to expand business and has based its telephone network on a system of fibre optic cables running alongside railway lines. Its main benefit over BT at present is cost, with Mercury claiming savings of 20 per cent on a telephone bill and even greater savings on local calls. While BT charges by the minute, Mercury charges by the second. Mercury also provides a comprehensive itemised bill which can be helpful to a company in monitoring and managing its telephone system. (This service can also be obtained from BT on request.)

Mercury offers three main services for the business and domestic user as well as the Centrex service which is available to customers on the London network. Each service is slightly different and involves a different cost. The main one is the 2100 service which is available in most areas, needs no special equipment and is geared to large companies. The 2200 service is geared towards small- and medium-sized businesses with users requiring what is termed a 'smartbox' – an interface between the telephone system and the public exchange in order to access Mercury lines. This smartbox is, however, an intelligent device so there is no need for the user to make a decision to use the Mercury network nor is there any need for a special code. Finally, the 2300 service is designed mainly for domestic users who need a Mercury-compatible telephone and are required to press a special 'M' button to route trunk calls via the Mercury network.

A recent White Paper on telecommunications proposes ending the duopoly held by BT and Mercury over the past decade by allowing competition from other companies. It is hoped that a more open policy, which would require the sanction of Parliament, will result in improved telecommunications services.

## Facsimile

This communication medium is now second only to the telephone and is an excellent method of sending urgent orders, diagrams or documents requiring signatures. A faxed order or booking, which can be sent in seconds, is generally accepted as being equally valid as its posted counterpart and can be a life-saver when time is short.

One tip with fax machines. Did you know that an empty fax machine will appear to be 'reserved' (the fax term for engaged)? If you have been trying to transmit to a fax number for some time, it may be worth phoning the company concerned and asking them to check whether their machine has run out of paper. By the same token, if *you* are responsible for a fax machine, make sure that paper is replenished regularly, particularly if you receive faxes after office hours. More about fax machines in Chapter 9.

## Telex

Before electronics had a hand in communications, the telex was the wonder invention providing the means of transmitting information via telephone lines, near and far. The impact was huge and lots of far-away places suddenly became very close. A description of the latest telex services (and teletex) is given in Chapter 9. However, here is a useful tip if you still have the old-fashioned telex machine.

Did you know that it's possible to have a telex conversation? Instead of preparing a message tape, call up the number and type your question directly. If the machine is attended, the recipient will be able to type back the answer and you can even proceed with a discussion. This is obviously more time-consuming and expensive than running through a tape at high speed (you can't correct errors either). However, if phone calls are difficult and only a brief exchange takes place, then it's magic. Some years ago, I had to make urgent contact with clients in a war-torn part of Africa. Even when the phones were out of order, we could have telex conversations and maintain essential communications. This system is also good for booking hotel rooms worldwide for the same reason.

## Expenses

Every company has its own method of dealing with executive expenses but, from your point of view, anything concerned with money (especially your boss's) should be dealt with promptly. There is nothing worse than wading through a pile of expenses months after they were incurred. Your boss will be niggled at having to rack his memory, and something is bound to be forgotten. You will also incur the wrath of the accounts department.

Try to keep an ongoing record, therefore, of every penny spent. Directly your boss returns from appointments, check to see if he has spent any money (taxis, fares, lunch costs etc). Note all the details in the office diary against the appropriate day. Retrieve any receipts or credit card slips and store these carefully. At the end of your expense accounting period it should be straightforward to draw up the accounts from the records you have. You'll also have the necessary receipts. What could be easier?

If your boss makes an overseas trip, give him a 'receipt' envelope with his foreign exchange and with luck he'll return with it bulging. Go through the envelope as soon as you can and clear any IOUs or petty cash advances he may have had.

*Chapter 5*

# Organisational Aspects

## Meetings

Secretaries spend a large part of their time organising gatherings. These can take the form of:

- One-to-one appointments;
- Meetings;
- Business lunches and dinners;
- Client presentations;
- Social occasions, such as retirement or leaving parties.

The same procedures have to be followed irrespective of the type of function and I shall therefore give an organisational checklist which applies to them all. I will then go through each function and mention some of its specific points.

Organising conferences and seminars is a topic all of its own (see page 71). Much help will be obtained from *How to Organise Effective Conferences and Meetings*, published by Kogan Page.

### Meeting organisation checklist

- Ring relevant secretaries and request appointments with their bosses, stating the reason why. Obtain several suitable dates and times. Ascertain what is definitely *not* possible in case you need to do a subsequent reshuffle. Knowing in advance what can and can't be done will save endless phone calls. (Booking by computer is dealt with on page 67.)
- Once you have an agreed date and time, book a suitable venue, taking account of the meeting's purpose. You obviously wouldn't book a confidential chat for two in the board room. *Put the booking in writing.*
- Ring the secretaries back and give verbal confirmation of the meeting date, time and venue. *Put in writing.*
- Contact the catering department and book refreshments if necessary (coffee, lunch, tea), taking account of any personal preferences, eg if the MD only drinks lemon tea. *Put this in writing.*

If the catering responsibility falls upon you, see the note on refreshments (page 69).

- Ensure that background papers and information are circulated to meeting attenders well in advance. If someone has to make a speech, make sure he knows about this in good time.
- If the meeting is in-house, check the venue on the appointed day. Ensure that it's clean and tidy; that there are pads and pencils, ashtrays and fresh drinking water.
- Keep copies of confirmatory details in your bring forward system – they are your alibi if anything goes wrong.
- Once the meeting is under way, there shouldn't be any interruptions. However, if something urgent crops up, take a typed message into the meeting room and pass it to the appropriate person. It takes courage to confront a sea of serious faces. Take a deep breath, put on a smile – and hope your boss is sitting near the door.

If you have a computer with a diary management program and have to arrange an internal meeting, you can achieve most of the preceding steps at the touch of a button. For the uninitiated, executive diary information is fed into a central processor by all secretaries. When a meeting has to be arranged, the computer will search through its files and find the most suitable date. Having done this, it will confirm the meeting, book the venue and remind the secretary to track down meeting papers. The system does, of course, rely on the quality of its information, and secretaries need to keep it fully updated on manually arranged appointments. Despite the inevitable loss of human contact, the computer can save hours of time spent on manually arranging and rearranging meeting dates.

Going back to the manual system, if someone who is not a 'regular' calls to request that your boss attends a meeting, take all the details and ring back with dates. You can then check with your boss whether he wishes to attend. If well up the executive ladder, he's likely to be bombarded with requests and will probably be very selective with his time. Of course, if the chairman's secretary calls, you co-operate immediately.

If you have to take meeting notes, arm yourself with a good supply of pens, pencils and note pads, and settle down for a busy time. You obviously don't have to make a verbatim account of all that is said. However, you do need to record the important points, as well as any action to be taken and by whom.

Type up your shorthand notes while they are still fresh in your mind. Draw up a rough draft (unless you're an old hand). There should be a separate 'Action' column down the right-hand side of each page into which you note relevant details. Let your boss check the rough through and then produce the final version – well before the next meeting date.

## General meetings

Having been through the general organisational procedures, we can now move on to more specific points:

*One-to-one appointments* (the easiest of all)

Appointments outside the office should be organised so that your boss makes the best use of time. For example, if he's already lunching in the City, it obviously makes more sense to book another appointment in the same location either just before or after lunch. Save him from as much cross-town travelling as you can.

If you have a visitor who overruns on time, you might have to effect a rescue. Buzz through to your boss, or put your head around his office door, with a reminder about his impending 'next appointment'. Even someone with the thickest skin should take the hint.

*Business lunches and dinners*

A carefully planned business meal can make all the difference to the conclusion of a tricky deal. When it comes to food, do your homework well and attend carefully to all details.

To return to the organisation checklist, plan the meal venue carefully, bearing in mind that people's tastes in food differ widely. To avoid complications with ethnic or religious differences, I'd always recommend somewhere plain. So many business people have to eat their way through rich and elaborate meals that excellent plain food should come as a refreshing treat. However, it obviously does depend on the occasion, so discuss this carefully with your boss.

In-house functions are always more straightforward (providing you have an efficient catering manager). You're on the spot to approve menus and wines, and can easily keep an eye on all the arrangements.

If arranging a formal function in a hotel, go along and see the venue yourself. Make your requirements very clear and put everything in writing. Never assume that oral assurances will be enough (they should be, of course, but always assume the worst).

You may have to pay extra for table flowers, special linen, Christmas crackers (if it's that time of year) etc. Check these details carefully. You don't want a nasty shock when the bill comes in.

Think about transport, before and after the meal (particularly if it's likely to be long and alcoholic). Pre-arranged cars will make your guests feel like royalty, especially if it's raining.

If there are a large number of guests, it is an idea to produce a table plan. Discuss this carefully with your boss.

*Client presentations*

The organisation of client presentations must go like clockwork. When your company is selling itself in a bid for business, the smallest hitch in arrangements can give a poor impression.

Check well in advance that you have all the necessary equipment and that it is working properly. This may include:

- Projectors;
- Screens;
- Flip charts;
- Transparency acetates and marker pens.

Give a list of clients to your receptionist so she can make them specially welcome. Organise a coat rack if it's winter.

If the presentation is a long one, make sure that empty cups are removed from the conference room during scheduled breaks. Empty the ashtrays, replenish drinking water and straighten chairs. Unless it is bitterly cold, open the windows and let in some fresh air. These little touches can make all the difference.

Consider stationing a desk outside the conference room for a secretary to take messages etc.

## DIY meeting refreshments

Providing liquid refreshments for a meeting should be straightforward – the secret is to plan ahead.

*Tea and coffee*

It is very difficult to manoeuvre a trayful of brimming cups gracefully, particularly when you have unsteady hands and closed doors to negotiate. I would therefore recommend that you take the tea or coffee tray into the venue before the meeting starts. Make sure you have all the cups, saucers, spoons, milk, sugar (and lemon) you'll need, plus extras. People have a habit of dropping into meetings. Put the milk jug(s) and sugar bowl(s) on the table within reach of everyone.

Thus prepared, you need only take the tea or coffee pot into the meeting when needed. Pour cups of black tea or coffee, and pass them around. People can help themselves to milk and sugar. Refill the pot and leave it on the tray. This is a discreet method of serving hot drinks which won't disturb the meeting. It's also easier on the nerves.

*Cold drinks*

When it comes to alcohol, you'll have to take orders individually. If there is a cocktail or drinks trolley in the meeting room then you can do this easily. If not, you will have to take a written order like a waitress and

bring the drinks later. It's courteous to ask if people would like ice and/
or lemon with appropriate drinks.

Unless you are skilled with a corkscrew, don't attempt to open a bottle
of wine in the meeting room. You'll probably end up hot and bothered
with a disintegrated cork. Find an adept colleague who'll do the job for
you.

Have a good supply of chilled fruit juice and other soft drinks for those
who prefer to avoid alcohol.

*Food*

If you have to cater for a working lunch without so much as a plate to
your name, don't despair. It's amazing what can be achieved with the
aid of your local sandwich shop or delicatessen (see Yellow Pages). Ring
around for an instant buffet. Many of these shops will not only prepare
and deliver the food (on silver salvers), but will also lend crockery and
cutlery (for a fee). They will probably bring cheese and fruit for dessert,
but if not you can always go round to your local supermarket. De luxe
paper napkins are a nice touch.

With sufficient notice you could engage professional caterers (subject
to the budget and occasion). There are hundreds of such specialists who
will cater for almost any kind of function.

## Social occasions

Although they shouldn't be, these are the very worst kind of function to
arrange because you can never please everyone. (Anyone who has
arranged a staff Christmas party will know what I mean.) However
smoothly things go, some bright spark will find fault with something. So
if faced with this daunting task, grow a few extra inches of skin and put
on your bravest smile. See Chapter 8 for tips on the Christmas party.

One of the most time-consuming social functions to arrange is a
leaving party. Not only are there the ordinary arrangements to consider,
but you also have to think about a staff collection and gift. Although
pleasantly sociable, going around with a collection takes ages and should
be delegated to a junior secretary if at all possible. Get an appropriate
card and ask all contributors to sign. Those located outside the building
can write their message on an adhesive label. This saves sending the card
all over the place.

I would always recommend asking the leaver what present he'd like.
If he wants to be 'surprised', ask for a list of preferred gifts at various
prices, which gives the best of both worlds. Allow plenty of time for gift
wrapping (unless the shop will do it for you). This is another time-
consuming task, especially if you have to tie the bows.

Arrange for someone suitable to make the formal gift presentation. This could be an immediate superior, head of department or personnel executive. If the person leaving is not very well known to him, supply brief biographical details on which he can base his remarks. These should include:

- Age;
- Length of service;
- Special achievements while with the company;
- Personal strengths;
- Future plans.

## Conferences and seminars

What is the difference? A *conference* is a consultation meeting, while a *seminar* is a conference of specialists. Although it's fatal to generalise, I tend to assume that conferences are large-scale events while seminars are small and select. However, if asked to organise either of these functions, prepare yourself for some hard work. What are the essential steps?

### Some months ahead

- *Find your venue.* Many hotels, leisure and entertainment complexes have conference facilities but these often get booked up months in advance (particularly around the Christmas period). So plan well ahead.

  How can you track down the right location? The purpose of the conference should be carefully considered when looking for a venue. For example, some sales conferences are held with the dual purpose of imparting information and giving company reps a pat on the back. Spouses could also be included in such a mixture of business and pleasure. You could therefore find yourself scouting around some exotic locations seeking the right blend of facilities. On the other hand, if organising a straightforward one-day seminar, the location's convenience (eg near a railway station) may be more important than any specialised services the venue can offer.

  If looking in the UK you could consult:

  *The Conference Blue Book*, which is the technical guide to conference venues in the British Isles, published annually by Benn Business Information Services. This lists over 2500 meeting venues indexed regionally and alphabetically by town. Descriptions and room plans are given for over 300 venues.

71

*The Conference Green Guide*, which is the special interest guide to conference venues in the British Isles, also published by Benn Business Information Services. It features over 800 conference venues which either offer special sports and leisure facilities or have amenities which are of particular historic or architectural interest.

Both these publications should be available in your reference library. If you wish to buy them, contact: Benn Business Information Services, PO Box 20, Sovereign Way, Tonbridge, Kent TN9 1RQ; tel 0732 362666.

The British Association of Conference Towns runs a free matching service between conference organisers and venue specialists throughout England, Northern Ireland, Scotland, Wales and the Channel Islands. To use the service and obtain a comprehensive conference compendium (free), contact: British Association of Conference Towns, 1st floor, Elizabeth House, 22 Suffolk Street, Queensway, Birmingham B1 1LS; tel 021-616 1400; fax 021-616 1364.

If you are planning an international conference, things may be trickier simply because of the choice available. Assuming that you have an idea of the particular country, you could contact that country's national airline who will probably have a conference department. Even if you don't want them to handle all the arrangements, they are probably an excellent place to start for advice.

Many of the international hotel chains will organise conferences for you. Some have a central reservations/enquiry service in the UK.

While you obviously cannot trail around looking at every potential conference venue, do take the trouble to visit those on your 'short list' or have them vetted by someone trustworthy. Skilful promotional literature may look wonderful, but can sometimes be misleading (like some holiday brochures).

- *Establish the budget* for the conference and work out your essential or 'fixed' costs (insurance, transport, venue, speakers etc) and then the extras or 'variable' costs (accommodation, entertainment etc). Ensure that the budget is approved before proceeding further.
- *Draw up the conference programme* with as many details as possible, including timing. Timing will be affected by the number of delegates, so it is important to have an approximate idea of attendance as early as possible.

- *Invite appropriate speakers* giving them full details of what is required of them and agree, specifically:

  — The subject matter of their speech and how it relates to the conference's purpose;
  — Speech timing;
  — Any audio-visual material they'll need to bring (ensuring that their material is compatible with the equipment available);
  — Accommodation/transport details;
  — Their fees and when they are payable.

- *Arrange for interpreters* if necessary. There are two kinds of conference interpretation:

  — *Simultaneous*, where interpreters sit in soundproof booths, listening to speeches through headsets and interpreting into a microphone at the same time.
  — *Consecutive*, where interpreters sit at the conference table, making notes of individual speeches. At the end of each statement, they repeat what has been said in the other language(s). This is mainly for small gatherings.

AIIC (International Association of Conference Interpreters) is the only organisation in the world representing conference interpreters which has formal agreements with the UN, EC and other international associations.

The UK branch of AIIC will arrange professional interpreters, working on a standard contractual basis, in accordance with your specific needs. There is a small administrative charge for this service. Interpreters' fees vary in accordance with the country of assignment. For further details contact: AIIC (British Isles), 46 Theobalds Road, London WC1X 8NW; tel 071-404 8847; fax 071-404 3164.

Alternatively, the Conference Interpreters Group are a co-operative of AIIC-registered interpreters who will attend national and international conferences. Contact them at: The Conference Interpreters Group, 10 Barley Mow Passage, London W4 4PH; tel 081-995 0801; fax 081-742 1066.

- If a public conference, *arrange for appropriate publicity* ensuring that registration details are displayed prominently.
- If a private conference, *write to prospective delegates* with programme details. Give a final registration date.
- *Arrange for the printing* of promotional literature such as:

  — Programme folders (personalised?);

— Name badges;
— General conference stationery;
— Conference registration forms.

Tell the printers to stand by for the printing of the programme when finalised.

- Decide if any *special events* are to be organised in conjunction with the conference, eg gala dinner, and get arrangements under way.

## Nearer conference time

- *Confirm delegate numbers.* Contact those who haven't replied and check their attendance.
- See if delegates will need:

    — Hotel accommodation;
    — Transport to and from venue;
    — Special facilities, eg wheelchairs if disabled.

- *Contact venue* and bring them up to date with the latest arrangements. Begin detailed plans such as menus, reception area, signposting etc. Confirm final numbers and make any overnight bookings.
- *Arrange for transport.*
- *Confirm delegate names to printers* for personalised stationery/programmes and/or name badges.
- *Arrange any personal itineraries*, eg if a delegate's spouse will be going riding nearby.
- *Prepare the final programme* and submit this to the printers (or word processing operator).
- *Send out the printed programme* to the delegates with any final instructions, venue location plans, timetables etc.
- *Contact speakers* and ensure their plans are proceeding. Send them a finalised programme with timing details. Arrange a venue rehearsal.

In overseas venues, much of this work must be left to a local agent or the professional organiser.

## Just before conference

- *Visit venue again* and check carefully:

    — Conference room layout;
    — Signposting;
    — Availability of delegate telephones and a message system;

— That a registration area has been set up, manned by conference experts;

— Final details on food and refreshments;

— Fire, safety and security procedures.

● Have the speakers' rehearsal, using the audio-visual equipment provided.

## The big day

● Get up early.
● Run through all arrangements again with the venue manager or co-ordinator.
● Check the conference room again and make sure that each delegate has pens, pads, water, ashtray (if smoking is allowed).
● Ensure that the audio-visual equipment is working.
● Put spare copies of conference literature on one side in case of emergencies.
● Be at the registration area in plenty of time and help welcome delegates – hand out folders and name badges.
● Expect to run a thousand errands.
● Stay on site until the conference is over.
● Check and confirm all accounts and bills while on site.

## Afterwards

● Write thank-you letters to all suppliers and speakers.
● Prepare and send out conference proceedings and/or speech texts if appropriate.
● Pay speakers.
● Deal with any complaints, or anything that went wrong (and get a satisfactory answer).

The British Tourist Authority produces a number of free leaflets which will be useful to those organising an international conference in Britain. These are: 'A Guide to Conference Marketing', 'Hosting an International Conference', and 'Country Conference Hotels' which can be obtained from BTA at: Thames Tower, Black's Road, Hammersmith, London W6 9EL; 081-846 9000; telex 21231; fax 081-563 0302.

If organising conferences on a regular basis you may like to join the Association of Conference Executives (ACE). This non-profit making organisation provides an international forum for the meetings industry and a comprehensive information service for its members.

Benefits of membership include a regular newsletter, training courses, social events, inspection visits, discount offers, regional meetings, seminars with an exhibition of services, insurance arrangements and publications such as the annual *ACE Buyers Guide*. The Association also has an arrangement whereby the magazine *Conference and Exhibition Fact Finder* is supplied to members.

For further details contact: The Association of Conference Executives, Riverside House, High Street, Huntingdon, Cambs PE18 6SG; tel 0480 457595; telex 32376; fax 0480 411341.

*Conference and Exhibition Fact Finder* is a monthly magazine which now incorporates the former ACE magazine, *Conference and Association World*. It is published by Batiste Publications Ltd, Pembroke House, Campsbourne Road, Hornsey, London N8 7PE; tel 081-340 3291; telex 267727; fax 081-341 4840.

Another useful publication aimed at conference and exhibition organisers is *Conference and Incentive Travel* which contains authoritative reportage on venues, services and technology. Copies of the magazine are available free to qualified readers from: *Conference and Incentive Travel*, Circulation Department, Haymarket Business Publications Ltd, 30 Lancaster Gate, London W2 3LP; tel 081-943 5000; fax 071-413 4514.

## VIPs

Any kind of guest comes within the category of a very important person and, as such, should receive every courtesy.

When making arrangements for VIPs, get as many details as you can:

- What is the purpose of their visit?
- What do they want to achieve?
- Will there be a social element to the visit?

If you find that the trip is a mixture of business and pleasure you will have quite a tall order. Many spouses accompany business travellers and you will probably end up as a courier.

If your visitors are from overseas, contact the relevant Tourist Board (see Chapter 6) and obtain the information about places and British events of interest. Unless you have to make specific bookings in advance, put these guides with other information to await the VIPs' arrival. If you have a stream of overseas visitors, it's a good idea to keep stocks of guidebooks on hand – you never know when they might come in useful.

Keep tabs on theatre review pages and be in a position to suggest good shows and plays in the locality. Find out about any festivals in your area. Develop relationships with your local booking agencies who will be able to get last-minute tickets for you.

A copy of *The Good Food Guide* will be useful if the VIPs wish to undertake some private experimentation with UK cuisine. The guide gives general information on recommended restaurants, hotels and pubs in the UK, with an indication of prices.

Having briefed yourself generally, get down to the specific programme:

- *Accommodation.* Ascertain what kind of hotel the VIP favours and do your best to book accordingly. Ensure it's in the right price bracket.

  Confirm the hotel reservation in writing and explain the method of payment. If the VIP is a company guest, ask for the bill to be sent to you. Confirm expected time of arrival.

  Should arrival be late at night, make arrangements with the hotel for a light meal (unless they have a 24-hour coffee shop or room service). Your VIP won't thank you if he has a sleepless night because of hunger pangs. Of course, if he has been on a long flight, he'll probably be sick of light meals, but you can never be sure.

  If necessary (and reasonable) take the trouble to inspect the hotel accommodation and make sure it's everything you thought. Leave a copy of the finalised itinerary (see page 87), tourist guides and other information at Reception. If the VIP does not have a car at his disposal, include relevant transport timetables, hire cab numbers and local maps.

  Fruit and flowers in the hotel room are a welcoming touch, particularly if there is a lady involved. Arrange for some daily newspapers. These are useful if only to check on that night's TV programmes.

- *Transport.* You may have to arrange for chauffeur transport for the duration of the stay. If you don't have a local contact, most of the large car rental chains will arrange this for you (see Chapter 6). Request a chauffeur with local knowledge and brief him personally. His will be an extremely important role – particularly if the VIP's English is a bit limited. Give him a copy of the finalised itinerary.

  In any event, arrange for the VIP to be met on arrival by someone from the company and taken to the hotel. Nothing is worse than struggling for taxis in a strange country when you have luggage and jetlag to contend with. The same applies to departure. These simple courtesies will leave him with a good impression of your firm.

- *Appointments.* Brief those people meeting the VIP. Do a formal résumé of his background if possible and include notes of each particular meeting's purpose. Ensure each person knows:

  — How long they have with the VIP;

— Where he's come from and is going to (and how he's going to get there).

Remember refreshments, and ensure that the VIP is fed and watered en route. Clarify any eating 'peculiarities' if these are known to you.

Draw up a formal itinerary (see Chapter 6), and a separate one for his wife if necessary. Send this to him well before his departure date. You'll then have time to make any necessary changes.

Arrange for the VIP to visit you and/or your boss at the start of his stay to discuss the finalised itinerary.

If the visit is a lengthy one, make periodic checks with the VIP to see that all is going well. Give him a list of emergency telephone numbers (just in case).

## Organising your boss

Depending on his character and style of work, keeping your boss organised will either be a pleasure or an unrelenting uphill task. Of course, he may not want to be organised (some people genuinely don't need it and others don't know what's good for them). Whether he does or not will depend on his:

- *Attitude*. If a bit old-fashioned, he may think you are stepping out of line. With patience, tact and amazing efficiency, you'll be able to soften this attitude in time.
- *Seniority*. Top executives have probably learnt through experience what a difference some secretarial organisation can make to their working lives. Many junior managers just don't have a clue (especially when newly promoted) and need to be 'trained' – diplomatically, of course.
- *Pressure of work*. If really pushed, he'll be only too pleased to know that someone else is in control.
- *Own organisation*. If well organised and methodical, he may only need occasional reminders. However, a boss like this shouldn't make you lazy. Your organising skills will have to be channelled into other directions, eg handling some of his routine tasks.

You will therefore have to weigh up the situation carefully.

In this sensitive area a gradual approach is usually best, although there are exceptions. Some bosses want to be organised from day one and if you are an experienced secretary, you'll be able to cope. However, if you are a novice or uncertain, take things gradually. Prove yourself in your own area and slowly extend your role.

Be unobtrusive and tactful. When approaching a new task it may be best if you make suggestions, rather than blundering in on something sacred. However, don't become so cautious that you don't use your initiative. Try to strike a balance.

## Planning his day

An important task of the secretary is to plan her boss's day sufficiently well so that his time is fully used. How is this achieved?

- Plan the diary in accordance with what he does best when. For instance, if he prefers to deal with paperwork first thing in the morning, try to organise meetings and appointments for the afternoon. However, you'll obviously have to be flexible on this – there has to be give and take in all meeting arrangements.
- Try not to cram meetings and appointments in one after the other. Unless he is a superman, your boss will need a bit of time between each to catch up on himself. Sensible spacing also allows a margin of error in case meetings overrun (and they usually do).
- To recap on the meetings checklist, book external meetings carefully, ensuring that cross-town travel is minimised.
- When returning from a business trip (or holiday) give him time to catch up. Try to keep the diary clear for his first working day – he'll probably have a mountain of post to go through. Don't book a lunch date unless it is essential – he'll probably be suffering from jetlag and may feel a bit anti-social.
- If your boss is under pressure with a specific project, eg writing a long report, try to keep him clear of anything other than urgent appointments. He'll need a certain amount of 'uncluttered time' in which to gather his thoughts.

## General

- Make sure your boss is well briefed on:

  — *Meetings and appointments*. Does he know where he is going and why? When arranging an external appointment somewhere unfamiliar, get full details of the location and how to reach it. Brief the chauffeur (if he has one), or photocopy a map if he's going under his own steam. Check on parking or train times. Arrange for him to be met at the station if necessary.

  To recap on the meetings checklist, ensure that your boss has all the relevant information he needs before any meeting. This may include papers and/or background data. Ensure this is

79

readily available and that he has more than five minutes in which to digest the facts. Book him some diary time if necessary.
— *Visitors*. Give him biographical information/background details on anyone new he is to meet.
— *Situations*. Top executives can often become isolated from their staff and office problems. I'm not suggesting that you run to him with office gossip, or become a spy, but there are times when it might be necessary for you tactfully to bring something important to his attention. Subordinates often grumble to the boss's secretary and while you should never betray a genuine confidence, you may have been told in the hope that you would have a judicious word. However, tread warily and think carefully before you speak.

● Establish a reporting system so that you can keep tabs on his subordinates' holidays, trips etc. Try to make sure there is always adequate staff cover.
● By the same token, ensure that his boss knows about his general movements. Give his secretary copies of trip itineraries, holiday dates etc so she is kept informed.
● Remind him about deadlines well in advance. Note regular reporting times in the diary and mark down time for any work he has to do for these. Never nag, but tactfully ensure that your boss is aware of urgent priorities.
● Unless he prefers to work in chaos, keep his office tidy. Check supplies when he isn't there and stock up on the equipment and stationery. Keep his pencils sharpened and make sure the biros work. Change his desk calendar every day. Keep an eye on the drinks cabinet and replenish supplies regularly. Water the plants.
● Try to keep track of your boss. Always ask where he's going when he leaves the office (unless it looks as if he's en route for the loo). You never know when a crucial telephone call with come in.
● In consultation with his wife, make sure he sees the dentist, optician etc regularly. Someone I worked for hated the dentist, and his wife and I were forced to conspire to make him go. (This worked like a dream but we weren't popular.)
● Keep a good supply of his personal stationery for any private correspondence.

## Stepping into the boss's boots

After a time, you should have absorbed enough of your boss's style to handle routine tasks and act on his behalf when he isn't around. This is an interesting and challenging development of the secretarial role, and one well worth striving for. What points should be borne in mind?

## Routine/admin

While you can forget about board meetings, there are many routine/ admin tasks which you can handle for your boss. Take an interest in his work and offer (tactfully) to help with some of the basics, eg research for reports, statistics etc. Don't be put off by work of a technical/numerical nature – this can have a fascination all of its own. (Much to my surprise, some of the most interesting work I've ever done was on statistics about exploration oilwells.) Be flexible and do the work to the best of your ability – you'll probably find it becomes part of your regular job.

A word of warning here. While it's essential to be kept busy, don't take on so much that you're too overworked to cope (unless given an assistant to handle your routine). Try to strike a balance. By the same token, if your role develops to a great extent on a permanent basis, ask for a pay rise.

## Deputising

In some ways it's almost more important what you do when your boss is away than what you do when he's there. The business world doesn't come to a halt because he's out of town. You therefore need to be on the ball to handle the routine and urgent matters which arise in his absence.

Use your judgement and common sense to assess whether tasks are best handled by:

- *You.* Do whatever you feel is necessary. If unsure, have a word with your boss's deputy or a senior secretarial colleague – they should be only too pleased to give their advice. Type a brief note of your actions (unless trivial) for your boss to see on his return.
- *One of your boss's staff.* Brief him properly and ensure he reports back with the outcome (unless trivial). You'll then be able to type up a note for your boss.
- *Your boss.* If something crops up that only he can deal with, you may need to track him down and pass on the matter for his personal attention. Make sure you have any background information he might need when you make contact.

## New members of staff

There will be times when new members of staff join your department, either executives, secretaries or both. As you know yourself, first impressions are extremely important and a cool reception can get a new job off to a bad start. Your personnel department may handle most of the arrangements but if not, here are some items you may wish to arrange yourself:

- Make sure there is adequate office accommodation which is fully stocked with all necessary equipment. This can be the best kind of welcome.
- Brief existing staff about the new arrival – either informally, by putting a notice in the staff magazine, or sending round a memo.
- Senior executives may need a formal induction programme. Discuss this with your boss and make the necessary appointments, giving lots of time for each (see VIP section, page 76, for tips). Send the itemised schedule to the executive before his joining date together with any background information which may be helpful, eg subsidiary company reports, management plans etc.
- Arrangements for junior staff will probably be less formal. Take them around on their first day (or make sure someone else does) and introduce them to the other staff. If working for a large organisation, restrict this to relevant departments or they'll become totally confused. Make sure someone takes them to lunch and keeps an eye on them generally. Pop in to see them yourself every couple of days to make sure they're settling in well.

## Showing appreciation

In the rush of coping with office panics, never forget your manners (or those of your boss, to be more accurate). Remind your boss to dictate thank-you letters (or write them yourself) immediately after he's received any kind of hospitality or gift. Thank-you letters done the same day show appreciation and are a natural courtesy to be cultivated.

By the same token, the giving of small gifts and/or flowers is marvellous PR. If someone has worked particularly hard; helped with a difficult problem; got married; had a baby; been promoted; a small reward or even just a note of thanks or congratulation can do much to show appreciation. Make a few tactful suggestions along these lines if your boss is a bit slow in this respect.

## Planning your holiday

Don't become such a conscientious secretary that you completely plan your holidays around those of your boss to save him any 'inconvenience'. This can be tempting if you work for one of those people who has decided (quite unfairly) that they are allergic to temporaries. Provided you book with a reputable agency, temps are usually excellent and well accustomed to handling the over-sensitive boss.

Having said that, you'll obviously have to be flexible when making your holiday plans, and fit in with those of other secretaries if you share an office. But don't be too unselfish or you'll find your whole life is dominated by work.

Your personnel department may be really on the ball when it comes to organising holiday relief, or you may end up with the task yourself. If you do, ask around the office and see if another secretary has a boss on holiday at the same time as you – perhaps she'd be willing to stand in for you (if you do the same for her, of course). Alternatively, perhaps there is a former secretary, maybe retired, who could come in and cover for you on a freelance basis? These are avenues which are well worth investigating as these secretaries will be familiar with the office set-up.

If you do have to use a temp make the booking in plenty of time, and state any special requirements. If possible, have a day's overlap with her so that you can introduce her to your trembling boss and show her the ropes. If this is not possible, write a few notes on essentials which helps the temp who comes in 'cold'. It's a good idea to leave notes on essentials anyway; even the most efficient temp can't be expected to remember every verbal instruction, and the notes are always available for anyone else who takes over at short notice – should you be ill, for example.

Ask one of your colleagues to welcome her on the first morning (particularly if she's in an office on her own) and to act as a point of contact for her queries. Needless to say, leave things well organised and in apple pie order. Put office equipment manuals, office handbooks and phone lists on the desk so that she can find her way around.

Ask her to leave you a note of anything important which arises while you are away. You may prefer that she leaves the filing on one side so that you can catch up on ordinary matters when you return.

Having done all this, you can go away with a clear conscience and have a lovely holiday.

## Despatch and translation services

### Messengers and couriers

It's fair to say that these days it is possible to get anything anywhere – but at a price. You have only to look in the Yellow Pages and you'll see companies offering a variety of despatch services. These range from basic motorbike messengers to international couriers who will almost scale mountain peaks to reach their destination. You obviously have to pay for what you get, and the more complex the assignment the higher the cost.

83

In fact, it might even be worthwhile sending a junior member of staff to hand deliver the document. However, if you do decide to use professionals, it's worth getting several quotes as charges vary.

Consult your local Yellow Pages or Business Pages for a start. If entries in a rural directory seem a bit sparse, look in your local library at the Yellow Pages/Business Pages of Central London or the nearest big city – many of the larger firms will collect documents from all over the UK.

### Translation services

Unless you are an expert linguist or there is one in the company, you are bound to need a translator at some stage in your secretarial career. Again, consult the Yellow Pages or Business Pages. Many translation companies offer a prompt facsimile or telex service which is particularly useful if you're in the habit of receiving letters, faxes or telexes in strange languages.

If you have technical, scientific, commercial or literary translation work, you could contact the Institute of Translation and Interpreting. The members of this specialist body meet exacting requirements in the fields mentioned. You can call the Institute with details of your assignment and they will give you the name of a suitable translator (this service is free). Alternatively, if you frequently need a variety of translators, you may like to buy the Institute's *Directory of Translators and Interpreters* which costs £45 and is updated annually. It lists over 800 qualified translators, cross-referenced by subject and language.

For further information contact: The Institute of Translation and Interpreting, 318a Finchley Road, London NW3 5HT; tel 071-794 9931; fax 071-435 2105.

# Chapter 6

# All About Travel

Nothing sounds more glamorous than 'travel' but the reality, particularly in business terms, is very different. Long, tiresome journeys across countries, continents and time zones do nothing but add to the pressure of the trip's purpose – the meeting, conference or briefing. Unlike the tourist, the business traveller has to switch into top gear at journey's end, irrespective of the stresses encountered in transit.

Travel companies, and airlines in particular, are capitalising on the special needs of the business executive and will smooth such travellers on their way – at a price. The crucial role, however, is played by the secretary who, through careful planning, can ensure that all aspects of her boss's trip are a success. It's a big responsibility. One badly planned meeting or delayed transport can have a knock-on effect and ruin the complete schedule. This chapter will serve as a useful guide.

## Drawing up an itinerary

As much care should go into the planning of a day in London as a trip to the Far East lasting several weeks (although the latter will obviously be more complex).

First, formulate a draft trip itinerary bearing in mind the following:

- What is the trip's purpose? Your boss may have a string of meetings, a factory to visit or a reception to host (maybe all three). Make a list of what he wishes to do and approximately how much time he can spend on each appointment. When you've added on a bit extra for emergencies and late bookings, this will give you an idea of the trip's length. Allow for travel time and for 'lost hours' when crossing time zones.
- Consult his diary (and those of his companions if he's travelling with others) and find at least two possible dates for departure. Remember to leave him a bit of recovery time on his return to the office – particularly if he's travelling back in an easterly direction across time zones (the jetlag is worse).
- Have preliminary discussions with the people your boss is planning to see and check their availability during the identified trip periods.

Allow for the difference in overseas public holidays – most business desk diaries list these for the current year.

- Check the relevant timetables to find out what is feasible in travelling terms. If the trip is planned for peak time (during the holiday season and around Christmas), check seat availability with your travel agent.

Type up a draft itinerary and discuss with your boss how details should be finalised. Make a provisional list of extra appointments to be slotted in, schedule permitting.

You can now begin organising the trip proper along the following lines (details on each point are given later in the chapter):

- Check that your boss's passport is in order and that the renewal date does not fall while he is away from the UK;
- See if any visas are necessary;
- Arrange for any inoculations and/or malaria tablets well in advance, if possible;
- Book the appropriate flights and make seat reservations;
- Organise any other transport;
- Order currency and travellers' cheques, and ensure that credit cards are valid;
- Get in a supply of phonecards if your boss doesn't have a chargecard;
- Book accommodation;
- Organise his meetings and appointments.

When you've arranged all these, type up a final trip itinerary (a sample is given on page 87).

Always give full postal addresses, telephone and fax numbers. Include useful contacts with business/home addresses and phone numbers. You never know when your boss may have the odd emergency that even you can't help with. All times shown should be local. Note down the time change if there is one, eg –5 hours GMT, and give the dialling code for calling home.

When finalised, copies of the itinerary should be given to:

- your boss (and his wife);
- his boss;
- your boss's deputy;
- the co-ordinating secretary in the host country (if applicable).

Keep a schedule on your noticeboard until the trip is over. Always file old itineraries as they can be particularly useful when planning return visits.

## Sample itinerary

---

MR A N OTHER: TRIP TO NEW YORK
1–4 March 1993 inclusive


Tuesday 1 March 1993

|  | At office |
|---|---|
| 16.00 | Car at office for airport trip (Ambassador Cars: 000 1111) |
| 17.00 | Arrive Terminal 3, London Heathrow Airport |
| 18.00 | Flight to New York – ZZ 101 |
| 20.00 (local time) | Arrive John F Kennedy Airport, New York (–5 hours GMT) Car waiting (Super Cars: 111 1111) |

HOTEL: Manhattan Hotel
452 East 200th Street, New York, NY 10000
(0101 212 111 2222; fax 0101 212 111 3333)
Telex: 77 232323 MAHOTEL


Wednesday 2 March 1993

| 09.00 | Briefing meeting with Mr Ronald P Other, President Any Company Inc 450 East 200th Street (000 5555; fax 000 5566) |
|---|---|
| 12.45 | Car waiting |
| 13.00 | Lunch with Mr Chuck T Other & Ms Shirley S Other Any Restaurant 395 West 100th Street (111 5555; fax 111 5566) |
| 14.15 | Car waiting |
| 14.30 | Meeting with Miss Doris R Other, President Any Other Company Inc 724 East 200th Street (0000 6666; fax 000 6677) |
| 18.00 | Drinks reception at Delaware Room, Manhattan Hotel |


TO CALL IF TIME:

Mr James F Other, Executive Vice-President, ANO Company
824 Broadway, NY 11001 (111 5522; fax 111 5577)

Mr Warren G Other, Vice-President, Another ANO Company
725 Park Avenue, NY 11001 (111 9999; fax 111 9009)

---

Thursday 3 March 1993

| | |
|---|---|
| 08.00 | Car waiting |
| 09.00 | Factory visit to Any Other Manufacturing Company Inc<br>2555 West Lynwood Boulevard, Lynn Valley, NY 12222<br>(888 8888; fax 888 9999) |
| 13.00 | Lunch on site with Mr Davis P Other, Executive President |
| 14.30 | Car waiting |
| 16.00 | Debriefing meeting with Mr Ronald P Other, President<br>Any Company Inc<br>450 East 200th Street<br>(000 5555; fax 000 5566) |
| 18.30 | Car waiting at Manhattan Hotel |
| 19.00 | Dinner with Mr & Mrs Ronald P Other<br>Any Other Restaurant<br>395 West 200th Street<br>(222 7777; fax 222 7799) |
| 21.30 | Car waiting to return to hotel |

Friday 4 March 1993

| | |
|---|---|
| 08.00 | Car waiting |
| 09.00 | Arrive Happy Airways Terminal, John F Kennedy Airport |
| 10.00 | Flight to London – ZZ 102 |
| 22.00<br>(local<br>time) | Arrive Heathrow Airport, Terminal 3<br>Ambassador Car waiting (000 1111) |

TO CALL HOME FROM NEW YORK – 011 44

Telephone numbers in New York

Mr & Mrs Ronald P Other, 434 Westchester Drive, Glenwood, NY 11000
(777 9999) – home

Mr Chuck T Other, Anonymous Company Inc, 111 Park Avenue, NY 11100
(111 6666; fax 111 6677) – office

Ms Shirley S Other, Another Anonymous Company, 779 Broadway, NY 11001
(111 5511; fax 111 5599) – office

## Passports

British passports are valid for ten years and can be obtained (and renewed/amended) as follows:

- By some banks or travel agents who will make a small charge for the service.

  Thomas Cook's service covers foreign nationals working in the UK whose London Embassy has authority to renew passports.
- By postal application to one of the various passport offices:

  *London*
  Passport Office, Clive House, 70 Petty France, London SW1H 9HD; tel 071-279 3434
  *Belfast*
  Passport Office, Hampton House, 47–53 High Street, Belfast BT1 2QS; tel 0232 232371
  *Glasgow*
  Passport Office, 3 Northgate, 96 Milton Street, Cowcaddens, Glasgow G4 0BT; tel 041-332 0271
  *Liverpool*
  Passport Office, 5th Floor, India Buildings, Water Street, Liverpool L2 0QZ; tel 051-237 3010
  *Newport*
  Passport Office, Olympia House, Upper Dock Street, Newport, Gwent NPT 1XA; tel 0633 244500
  *Peterborough*
  Passport Office, Aragon Court, Northminster Road, Peterborough PE1 1QG; tel 0733 895555

  The nearest office is not necessarily the one to which you should apply. Details are given on application forms, available at the Post Office.

  Postal applications take at least four weeks, and up to three months between February and August.

  The current fees for basic passports are:

  up to 32 pages £15
  94 pages £30

- By personal application to a Passport Office between 9.00 and 4.30, Monday to Friday (except the London office which closes at 4.00). This method may mean queueing and does not guarantee priority treatment. Documents are either:

  — Left in a post-box where they are treated like postal applications;

— Handed in and checked, with the new passport being available or posted at a mutually convenient time.

It is only in extremely urgent circumstances that passports can be available within 24 hours. Return by registered post can be arranged provided you send £1.40 to cover the cost.

British Visitors Passports are valid for one year and must be obtained by the prospective holder *in person* from main post offices. Spouses and/or children to be included on the passport should accompany the holder when application is made.

Basic costs for these passports are £7.50 (£11.25 if spouse to be included). A Visitors Passport can only be used for holidays and unpaid business trips (of up to three months), and are not valid for countries requiring a visa.

Trips to France can now be made using a British Excursion Document available from all main post offices. This is valid for trips to France involving a stay of no more than 60 hours. Travel must be made on an excursion ticket where outward/return journeys are via the same airport/seaport. The fee for a British Excursion Document is £2.00.

## Vaccinations and visas

The following information on vaccinations and visas is reproduced by kind permission of British Airways.

---

Prevention is, of course, far better than cure. When you are travelling, particularly in tropical or sub-tropical climates, you run the risk of being in contact with infections and diseases you have little natural immunity against. So, well before travelling, check with your doctor what vaccine or vaccines you may need, and try to allow sufficient time for the vaccinations to take effect. It can be some days after vaccination before you are covered.

It is often not possible for your local doctor to get the necessary vaccines in time if you find that you have to take off at short notice. In that case, British Airways' immunisation facilities can be a lifesaver. The airline has generations of experience in the business of preventive medicine for travellers.

There are British Airways Travel Clinics throughout the UK where you can get any necessary vaccinations. Telephone 071-831 5333 (24 hours) for details of your nearest clinic. In London there are clinics at 156 Regent Street (071-439 9584); Little Newport Street, Leicester Square (071-287 2255/3366); 101 Cheapside (071-606 2977); Harrow (081-861 1181); Heathrow Airport (081-562 5825); and Purley (081-763 1372).

Most clinics are open daily and some operate on Saturday or in the evenings. Although you can often be seen at short notice, an appointment is recommended and no immunisation advice can be given over the phone.

The list below gives both current vaccination and entry requirements for British passport holders travelling to over 70 countries in the world.

As this information is subject to change, please contact British Airways Medical Services, your doctor or the embassy of the country you are visiting six weeks before departure (if possible).

The Medical Advisory Service for Travellers Abroad (MASTA) will, by return of post and for a £7 fee, prepare a personalised health brief based on their information bank covering 84 health hazards in 230 countries. Application forms are available from all branches of Boots, Savory & Moore and R Gordon Drummond, or from MASTA direct. MASTA also sells a wide range of travel health items (including AIDS and hepatitis B transmission prevention packs) by mail order or from them direct at: MASTA, London School of Hygiene and Tropical Medicine, Keppel Street, London WC1E 7HT; tel 071-631 4408.

## World vaccination and visa guide – what you need, and where

| *Vaccinations* | R = Recommended | | Yes = Necessary |
|---|---|---|---|
| *Visas* | M = May be required | | Yes = Necessary |

| | Cholera | Malaria† | Typhoid Polio | Y/fever | Visa |
|---|---|---|---|---|---|
| Algeria | R | R | R | | M |
| Australia | | | | | Yes |
| Bahamas | | | R | | |
| Bahrain | R | | R | | M |
| Bangladesh | R | R | R | | Yes |
| Barbados | | | R | | |
| Bermuda | | | R | | |
| Brunei | R | | R | | |
| Bulgaria | | | R$^T$ | | Yes |
| China | | R | R | | Yes |
| Cyprus | | | R$^T$ | | |
| Czechoslovakia | | | | | Yes |
| Egypt | R | R | R | | Yes* |
| Ethiopia | R | R | R | R | Yes |
| Germany | | | | | |
| Ghana | R | R | R | R | Yes |
| Gibraltar | | | R$^T$ | | |
| Greece | | | R$^T$ | | |

| | Cholera | Malaria† | Typhoid Polio | Y/fever | Visa |
|---|---|---|---|---|---|
| Guyana | | R | R | R | |
| Hong Kong | | | R | | |
| Hungary | | | | | Yes |
| India | R | R | R | | Yes |
| Indonesia | R | R | R | | Yes |
| Iran | R | R | R | | Yes |
| Iraq | R | R | R | | Yes |
| Israel | R | | R | | |
| Italy | | | R$^T$ | | |
| Ivory Coast | R | R | R | Yes | |
| Jamaica | | | R | | |
| Japan | | | R | | |
| Jordan | R | | R | | Yes |
| Kenya | R | R | R | R | M |
| Korea (South) | R | | R | | |
| Kuwait | R | | R | | Yes |
| Lebanon | R | | R | | Yes |
| Liberia | R | R | R | R | Yes |
| Libya | R | R | R | | Yes |
| Malawi | R | R | R | | |
| Malaysia | R | R | R | | |
| Malta | | | R$^T$ | | |
| Mauritius | | R | R | | |
| Mexico | | R | R | | Yes |
| Morocco | R | R | R | | |
| Mozambique | Yes | R | R | | Yes |
| Nigeria | R | R | R | Yes | Yes |
| Oman | R | R | R | | Yes |
| Pakistan | R | R | R | | M |
| Panama | | R | R | R | |
| Peru | | R | R | R | |
| Philippines | R | R | R | | Yes |
| Poland | | | | | Yes |
| Portugal | | | R$^T$ | | |
| Qatar | R | | R | | |
| Rwanda | R | R | R | R | Yes |
| Saudi Arabia | R | R | R | | Yes |
| Seychelles | | | R | | |
| Sierra Leone | R | R | R | R | Yes |
| Singapore | R | R | R | | |
| South Africa | R | R | R | | |
| Spain | | | R$^T$ | | |
| Sri Lanka | R | R | R | | Yes |
| Sudan | R | R | R | R | Yes |
| Syria | R | R | R | | Yes |
| Taiwan | R | | R | | Yes |
| Tanzania | R | R | R | R | Yes |
| Thailand | R | R | R | | Yes |
| Turkey | R | R | R | | |

| | Cholera | Malaria† | Typhoid Polio | Y/fever | Visa |
|---|---|---|---|---|---|
| Uganda | R | R | R | Yes | M |
| UAE | R | | R | | |
| USA | | | | | Yes |
| USSR | | | R$^T$ | | Yes |
| Yemen | R | R | R | | Yes |
| Yugoslavia | | | R$^T$ | | |
| Zambia | R | R | R | R | |
| Zimbabwe | R | R | R | | |

| | |
|---|---|
| R$^T$ | Typhoid only recommended |
| * | Passport should be valid for at least six months beyond period of stay |
| † | Anti-malaria tablets required |

At time of going to press, *no* vaccinations or visas are required for travellers from Britain to the following countries:

| | |
|---|---|
| Austria | Irish Republic |
| Belgium | Netherlands |
| Canada | New Zealand |
| Denmark | Norway |
| France | Sweden |
| Iceland | Switzerland |

For a complete country list of vaccination requirements and further information on health precautions while travelling abroad, see leaflet T1 'The Traveller's Guide to Health', obtainable free from the Department of Health. Yellow fever and other vaccination centres throughout the UK are also listed.

Some vaccinations are free under the NHS; for others there may be a charge. Doctors can also charge for signing or filling in a certificate. In addition to those already listed, there are a number of other commercial vaccination centres, at which charges may be payable:

Thomas Cook Travel Clinic
45 Berkeley Street, London W1A 1EB; tel 071-499 4000

Medical Department, Unilever House
Blackfriars, London EC4P 4BQ; tel 071-822 6017

Vaccinating Centre
53 Great Cumberland Place, London W1H 7LH; tel 071-262 6456

Hospital for Tropical Diseases
4 St Pancras Way, London NW1 0PE; tel 071-387 4411.

It is important to note that even though yellow fever vaccination is often only recommended, this would become mandatory if visiting two or more countries within the endemic zone.

## Malaria precautions

If your boss has to visit a country within the malaria belt at short notice, telephone the Malaria Reference Clinic (071-636 7921/8636) which has up-to-the-minute recorded information on anti-malarial drugs which need to be taken a week before departure and up to six weeks after returning to the UK. Advice can also be obtained from the Hospital for Tropical Diseases or British Airways Travel Clinic (tel 071-831 5333 to find your nearest BA centre). BA do stress, however, that expert medical advice should always be sought with regard to malaria, as the type of medication and dosage varies according to the country concerned and conditions prevailing at the time, as well as to the malaria mosquito's resistance to drugs in many areas.

## Medical insurance

If your boss is visiting a country in the EC get him to fill in form CMI (obtainable from the Department of Social Security). He will be issued with an E111 form which will provide him with free or reduced cost emergency treatment if he is suddenly taken ill. Also check that his medical insurance cover is up to date and adequate (companies usually provide this for travelling executives but small firms may not).

## Visas

A list of countries requiring visas is given on page 91. Double-check current requirements with your travel agent and/or direct with the appropriate embassy. There are three different ways to get a visa:

- Through a travel agent (who will probably charge a fee). Unless you are a 'regular' at embassies, this is probably the simplest method. Thomas Cook run a special visa service and will handle your requirements speedily. They have a special emergency service for short-notice trips.
- By postal application to the appropriate embassy. This method is fine if you are not in a rush, as visas obtained this way can take several weeks to come through.
- By direct application to the embassy. Assuming you're located nearby, this method may necessitate long hours in a queue. If the relevant country has no embassy in the UK, a trip to the nearest one in a European city may be necessary.

If your boss is visiting governmental agencies in a country where obtaining visas is difficult, it may be possible for the hosts to arrange for a visa to be available at the point of entry. In this instance you will certainly need to obtain a telex or other documentation confirming this, or the airline may well refuse passage.

## Booking flights

Competition is the name of the game in the travel industry and each airline spends a small fortune trying to convince the fare-paying public that its service is the best. How do you see through the slogans to make sure your boss is getting the best deal?

- An experienced business travel agent with an insight into your boss's own travel requirements will be a big help, of course;
- Some seasoned travellers have their own pet theories – such as using the national airline of the destination country where there may be preferential ground treatment.

However, before trying to sort the wheat from the chaff, there are a few basic facts which you should be aware of.

Generally speaking, there are three separate travelling classes on long-haul flights (apart from Concorde which is all first class):

- *Economy.* This is the tourist class where standard service is available (but is often used by business people). This usually includes complimentary food, drink and in-flight entertainment (often a film as well).
- *Executive* or *business.* This was introduced to meet the demand for an improved economy service at a reduction on the first-class fare. Seats in this part of the cabin are roomier than in tourist and spaced more generously. In addition to the standard service, there is often a choice of menu and a better selection of wines. Complimentary slipperettes, eye shades and even a gift are sometimes offered. There is a separate check-in desk on the ground and many airlines have their own executive lounges.
- *First class.* The best thing about first class is the seats! Most airlines now have 'sleeper seats' which allow passengers to stretch out completely (this makes all the difference on a long flight). Some airlines have a first-class section on the upper floor of their 747s.

    In addition to these facilities, first-class passengers enjoy a superior cabin service, several menu choices and separate check-in and baggage handling on the ground.

Airlines offer slight variations on the classes – the above is intended to serve as a guide only.

Some airlines have now dispensed with first class on short-haul flights because of falling demand. In a world recession many people feel unable to justify the extra cost of first-class fares on anything other than long-haul flights.

Concorde is, of course, in a class of its own. For little more than the first-class subsonic fare, it's possible to cross the Atlantic in about half the time (four hours on average). There is the superior cabin service you'd expect, and special check-in and baggage handling ensure that time saved in the plane is not lost on the ground.

There's more, too. Courtesy helicopters or cars will speed Concorde passengers from John F Kennedy Airport in New York to downtown Manhattan or to New York's two other airports – La Guardia or Newark. Special services such as these can be arranged on request at the check-in desk. What more could be needed to set up your boss for that special business appointment?

Unless your company has its own travel department, establish good relations with the business sector of a travel agent. Using their computer software they will be able to give you up-to-the-minute flight avail-abilities. When making reservations, stop to consider the following:

- Unless your boss is making a planned stopover en route, make sure you specify a *non-stop* flight when booking. This is distinct from a *direct* flight which often makes fuelling and/or passenger stops not always shown in the airline guide. Be very definite with your travel agent or you could come a cropper with this misleading bit of jargon (I speak from personal experience).
- Allow plenty of time between flights if a change of plane is necessary (no one can guarantee good flying weather).
- Bear in mind that flights into, within or from the Third World can be highly unreliable – allow for delays of up to 24 hours when making appointments. Allow time, too, for long journeys (owing to traffic congestion) to local airports, for example Lagos.
- Make sure that the planes arrive and leave from the same airport, as many major cities have several. If this can't be arranged, allow plenty of time for the coach or helicopter transit journey.
- If the chosen flight is fully booked, ask to be put on a 'wait-list' of standby passengers in case of cancellations. However, you should obviously make reservations on an alternative flight too in case the first choice stays booked.
- Ask the travel agent to reserve plane seats in accordance with your boss's preference: smoking or non-smoking; aisle, centre or window seats. Some airlines offer completely non-smoking flights.

  Many airlines now offer seat reservations to economy as well as executive and first-class passengers. Seat booking in advance gives greater choice and saves any last-minute fuss at check-in time. Boarding cards giving seat numbers will be issued with the plane tickets and all your boss needs to do at the airport is check in his baggage.

- Check with the travel agent whether reconfirmation of the return flight is necessary. Most airlines recommend that booked passengers should reconfirm their return journeys 72 hours before departure.
- Examine the plane tickets carefully and make sure they're in order. Put them in a safe place.

## Organising transport

Whether it's a chauffeured limousine or a humble rickshaw, nothing will ease your boss into his trip schedule so well as having local transport pre-arranged. Travelling around a strange city is a wearying business, particularly if you have just arrived from a long flight. Funds permitting, always organise the best possible transport available.

When organising a trip, therefore, think about each stage of the journey carefully and make appropriate arrangements (unless your boss always insists on taking taxis):

- Arrange for transport to take him to the airport and be there for the return flight (this is most important as he'll probably be exhausted by then). Passengers need to check in at least an hour before the flight leaves (and even more if you haven't been able to book seat reservations), so allow plenty of time. Use a reliable car hire firm who are accustomed to airport trips. Put all the details in writing if you have time and sufficient notice.

    There is some extremely efficient public transport linking major cities and airports these days, but speaking personally, I'd rather take my chances with the traffic (it's less likely to go on strike).
- Organise someone to meet him at the destination – perhaps a secretary in the company he's going to visit will advise you here. If not, many of the large car hire chains will arrange chauffeured cars on an international basis – contact your nearest branch for details.

    They will also be able to help if you should need to arrange for either a self-drive or chauffeured car for the trip's duration. Several of these companies operate a credit card system, so arrangements could not be easier.

## Money

Whether paper, travellers' cheques or bits of plastic, you need to ensure that your boss has sufficient funds to sustain himself on a trip.

- *Foreign exchange* and *travellers' cheques* can be obtained either from a travel agent or bank, both of which should be able to supply your needs within a few days. Allow extra time for unusual currency.

A list of currencies by country appears below. When ordering, request some small denomination notes. Nothing is more likely to result in a heavily inflated tip than presentation of a $100 billl to an airport taxi. If your boss makes regular overseas trips, keep any currency coins in the safe for him to take next time around (or beg these from other travelling executives in the company).

Travellers' cheques should be ordered in the local currency and never in sterling which can be surprisingly difficult to change abroad – even in North America.

For emergencies, there is a 24-hour bank at Heathrow Airport. Most other UK airports have banks with long opening hours, which are extended even further during the summer.

Keep a record of currency and travellers' cheques received and the prevailing exchange rate. This will be a big help when you come to do the trip expenses. If this should slip your mind, however, you can always check exchange rates in the relevant back copy of the *Financial Times*.

The following table is reproduced with the kind permission of *Business Traveller*.

## Countries and currencies

Afghanistan (Afghani)
Algeria (Dinar)
Antigua (CFD)
Argentina (New Peso)
Australia (Dollar)
Austria (Schilling)
Bahamas (Dollar)
Bahrain (Dinar)
Barbados (Dollar)
Belgium (Franc)
Belize (Dollar)
Benin (CFA)
Bermuda (Dollar)
Bolivia (Peso)
Botswana (Pula)
Brazil (Cruzeiro)
Brunei (Dollar)
Bulgaria (Lev)
Cameroon (CFA)
Canada (Dollar)
Chile (Peso)
China (Yuan)
Colombia (Peso)

Costa Rica (Colon)
Cyprus (Pound)
Czechoslovakia (Koruna)
Denmark (Krone)
Dominican Rep
  (East Caribbean Dollar)
Ecuador (Sucre)
Egypt (Pound)
Eire (Pound)
Fiji (Dollar)
Finland (Markka)
France (Franc)
Germany (Deutsche Mark)
Ghana (Cedi)
Gibraltar (Pound)
Greece (Drachma)
Guatemala (Quetzal)
Guyana (Dollar)
Honduras Rep (Lempira)
Hong Kong (Dollar)
Hungary (Forint)
Iceland (Krona)
India (Rupee)

Indonesia (Rupiah)
Iran (Rial)
Iraq (Dinar)
Israel (Shekel)
Italy (Lira)
Jamaica (Dollar)
Japan (Yen)
Jordan (Dinar)
Kenya (Shilling)
Korea (Won)
Kuwait (Dinar)
Lebanon (Lebanese Pound)
Liberia (Dollar)
Libya (Dinar)
Luxembourg (Franc)
Malagasy Rep (Franc)
Malawi (Kwacha)
Malaysia (Ringgit)
Malta (Pound)
Mauritius (Rupee)
Mexico (Peso)
Morocco (Dirham)
Netherlands (Guilder)
New Zealand (Dollar)
Nigeria (Naira)
Norway (Krona)
Oman (Rial)
Pakistan (Rupee)
Paraguay (Guarani)
Philippines (Peso)
Poland (Zloty)
Portugal (Escudo)

Qatar (Ryal)
Romania (Leu)
El Salvador (Colon)
Saudi Arabia (Ryal)
Seychelles (Rupee)
Sierra Leone (Leone)
Singapore (Dollar)
Somali Rep (Shilling)
South Africa (Rand)
Spain (Peseta)
Sri Lanka (Rupee)
Sudan (Pound)
Sweden (Krona)
Switzerland (Franc)
Syria (Pound)
Taiwan (Dollar)
Tanzania (Shilling)
Thailand (Baht)
Trinidad & Tobago (Dollar)
Tunisia (Dinar)
Turkey (Lira)
Uganda (Shilling)
United Arab Emirates (Dirham)
Uruguay (Peso)
USA (Dollar)
USSR (Rouble)
Venezuela (Bolivar)
Yemen (Rial)
Yugoslavia (New Dinar)
Zaire Rep (Zaire)
Zambia (Kwacha)
Zimbabwe (Dollar)

---

● *Credit cards* come into their own on business trips (particularly in North America) where plastic seems almost more acceptable than real money. Before making a trip, check your boss's cards and make sure he remembers to take them. If you get an SOS about lost or stolen cards, contact:

Access/Eurocard/Mastercard
Joint Credit Card Company, Access House, 200 Priory Crescent, Southend-on-Sea, Essex SS2 6QQ; tel 0702 352211
Ring the special Access number of the card issuing bank who operate a 24-hour service, then write a confirmatory letter within seven days.

Barclaycard/Visa
Barclaycard Centre, Department G, Northampton NN1 1SG; tel 0604 230230

Report the loss to any branch of the Barclays Group. Outside normal banking hours, call the Barclaycard Centre number on page 99. Write a confirmatory letter within seven days.

American Express Card
Lost & Stolen Department, PO Box 68, Edward Street, Brighton BN2 1YL; tel 0273 688363
Report the loss to American Express on the above number (24-hour service), then write a confirmatory letter within seven days. (Any other enquiries should be made by phone to 0273 696933 which connects directly to a customer service representative. Outside normal office hours an emergency line – 071-222 9633 is staffed 24 hours a day, 365 days a year.)

Diners Club Card
Diners Club House, Kingsmead, Farnborough, Hants GU14 7SR; tel 0252 516261
There is a 24-hour service for lost cards, which should be reported to the above number and then confirmed with a letter within seven days.

## Booking accommodation

When arranging hotel accommodation for your boss, remember it should provide an oasis of comfort at the end of a tiring day. How is this achieved?

- If making a return visit, he's likely to have his own hotel preference. If not, you can:

  — Get a personal recommendation for a good hotel central to his area of business, perhaps from your counterpart in the city concerned;
  — Consult one of the many international hotel guides which should be available at your local reference library (the *Financial Times* produces an excellent guide).

  If adopting the latter method, ensure that the chosen hotel is conveniently located. You can look at a city map either by obtaining one from the tourist board in this country, or by consulting one of the executive desk diaries which give international city maps in the back (eg *The Economist*).
- Having selected the right hotel, how do you make a reservation?

  — Your travel agent can arrange this for you;
  — You can book direct with the hotel by telephone, telex or fax

(ensuring that you send a confirmatory telex, fax or letter afterwards);
— You can contact one of the central reservations offices for the big international hotel chains which are normally located in London (a few are given at the end of this section). They will send you a computerised confirmation of the reservation once made. This service is usually free.

● Confirmatory reservation telexes or faxes should give the following information:

— Name and company;
— Duration of stay;
— Method of payment;
— Time of arrival;
— Any special requirements.

Time of arrival is most important as most hotels won't hold reservations after 6 pm unless they have written notification of a 'late arrival'.
● Should your boss be staying with friends or contacts:

— ensure you have sufficient details of his whereabouts;
— remind him (tactfully) that he may wish to take a gift.

### Central reservation offices
Here are just a few:

Best Western Hotels, Vine House, 143 London Road, Kingston upon Thames, Surrey KT2 6NA; tel 081-541 0050

Hilton International & Vista Hotels, 179–199 Holland Park Avenue, London W11 4UL; tel 071-603 3355

Holiday Inn Worldwide Reservation Office, 10–12 New College Parade, Finchley Road, London NW3 5EP; tel 071-722 7755

### Arranging meetings and appointments

Once you have organised the 'mechanics' of a business trip, it's time to arrange the meetings. As arrangements for these are pretty much the same wherever they're located, refer to the 'meetings' section in Chapter 5. However, there are a few extra points to remember when organising these for a trip:

● Your boss obviously needs to make the best use of his time away but it is a false economy to cram so much into his schedule that he comes back a nervous wreck. Travelling is extremely tiring, so show some consideration in booking his time. You also need to allow a certain amount of 'free' time so that he can write up appointments, make telephone calls and perhaps have the odd social engagement.

- Obtain city plans so that you know where he will be visiting. This will enable you to avoid booking cross-town appointments.
- Confirm meetings and appointments by telex, fax or letter (allow plenty of time if relying on air mail).

## General organisation tips

- Have all the papers needed for the trip ready well in advance, sectioned into clear plastic folders so that they are easy to see. Try to keep heavy documents to a minimum.
- As well as the above, ensure your boss also takes:

  Passport and visas;
  Tickets and money;
  Insurance details;
  Business cards;
  Personal organiser;
  Address book (pocket sized);
  Destination street maps if he's not being chauffeured;
  An envelope for his receipts and credit card slips;
  Dictating machine and plenty of tapes (to keep you busy on his return);
  A lined pad, pens and any other stationery he might need;
  Inoculation certificates (if necessary);
  Malaria tablets (if applicable);
  Personal medication (if applicable);
  Sleeping tablets if he uses these for jetlag;
  Telephone chargecard or phonecards (see below).

- Keep your fingers crossed and stay near a phone!

## General information

- Foster good relations with your travel agent. Call in and see him and have a frank exchange of views. An appreciation of each other's requirements, problems and limitations can be a big help when there's a panic on. Try to give your travel agent as much notice of future trips as possible (no one can perform miracles all the time).

  Over 5500 British travel agents are members of ABTA (the

Association of British Travel Agents). They must have a minimum number of staff who have certain qualifications and experience, and must abide by ABTA's code of conduct.

For further details, contact: Association of British Travel Agents, 55–57 Newman Street, London W1P 4AH; tel 071-637 2444.

- Check your company insurance plan and ensure that there is sufficient medical cover. (Further information on medical costs abroad can be obtained in leaflet T1 available from the Department of Health.)

  If making a company group booking, check your policy to see if there are restrictions on the number of executives travelling together. (You don't want to invalidate any subsequent claims.)

- World time differences can be found in the telephone books issued to all subscribers. You will see that time changes go up to a maximum of plus or minus 12 hours GMT at which point you reach the international date line. Check your schedule dates carefully if this is crossed in the course of a journey – it's quite possible to arrive somewhere the day before you left. (There are lots of funny stories about the date line: it once passed through a grocery shop in Fiji which gave the proprietor the best of both worlds as he only had to close half the shop on Sundays!)

- There are two business travel magazines which are full of useful information:

  *Executive Travel* is published monthly for regular travellers, company travel managers and IATA travel agents in the UK. It is carried aboard 20 international airlines and is available to guests at key UK hotels.

  Copies are on sale at newsagents or on subscription. For further information, contact: Executive Travel Magazine, Reed Travel Group, Francis House, 11 Francis Street, Victoria, London SW1P 1BZ; 071-828 8989.

  *Business Traveller* is published monthly and is a subscription magazine with an independent editorial policy. Every month experts offer advice on how to get the best current flight, hotel and travel deals. Insider's Guides and Destination Reports give invaluable information on business cities throughout the world.

  For further information, contact: Business Traveller, Perry Publications Ltd, 388–396 Oxford Street, London W1N 9HE; tel 071-629 4688; fax 071-629 6572.

- If your boss is a regular traveller, keep a record of his passport renewal and inoculation booster dates in the diary.

- Keep your boss supplied with BT phonecards to save him carrying large amounts of small change. A BT chargecard is even more useful because it can be used to make calls from *any* phone (including payphones) in more than 120 countries. The chargecard itself is free but call charges are slightly higher than conventional calls. Calls are charged to your company's quarterly bill. For full details of BT's chargecard or to obtain an application form, phone BT's Products and Services Department on 0800 800 855.

- The Air Transport Users' Committee is a consumer representative body for airline passengers and the shippers of air freight. It can help to resolve complaints against the providers of air services, airlines, travel agents, tour operators and freight forwarders. The AUC produce two excellent free leaflets: 'Flight Plan' (hints for airline passengers) and 'Care in the Air' (advice for handicapped passengers).

  For further information, contact: Air Transport Users' Committee, 2nd Floor, Kingsway House, 103 Kingsway, London WC2B 6QX; tel 071-242 3882; fax 071-831 4132.

- UK Tourist Boards are located as follows:

British Tourist Authority (provides general information on promoting Britain abroad), Thames Tower, Black's Road, Hammersmith, London W6 9EL; tel 081-846 9000

English Tourist Board, Thames Tower, Black's Road, Hammersmith, London W6 9EL; tel 081-846 9000

Wales Tourist Board, Brunel House, Fitzalan Road, Cardiff CS2 1UY; tel 0222 499909

Scottish Tourist Board, 23 Ravelston Terrace, Edinburgh EH4 3EW; tel 031-332 2433

Northern Ireland Tourist Board, River House, 48 High Street, Belfast BT1 2CF; tel 0232 231221

London Tourist Board, 26 Grosvenor Gardens, London SW1W 0DU; tel 071-730 3488.

*Chapter 7*

# Research

You never know when you might need to lay your hands on specialised information. During my secretarial career I've had to research all sorts of things so I know a brief guide to reference sources will be useful. First, however, here are a few tips on conducting research:

- *Consult the experts.* Life is too short to go over well-trodden ground. There are trade associations and/or professional bodies covering almost every subject imaginable, most of whom will have a PR department only too pleased to give information. These organisations can be located in the Yellow Pages or Business Pages, or by reference to:

    *Directory of British Associations & Associations in Ireland*
    7th edition, 1982, published by CBD Research Ltd

    ASLIB *Directory of Information Sources in the UK*
    Vol. 1 – Science, Technology & Commerce
    Vol. 2 – Social Sciences, Medicine & the Humanities
    5th edition, 1984, published by the Association for Information Management

    ASLIB *Economic & Business Information Group Membership Directory*, edited by M Rasdall and H Lambert, published by TFPL Publications.

    *Hollis Press & Public Relations Annual*
    gives press contacts on all manner of subjects, plus useful organisations and PR companies.

- *Seek out the reference librarian.* These helpful people are usually mines of information on practically anything. Unless your subject matter is very specialised and likely to have a library of its own, contact your local reference library. The British Library is, of course, the national collection and information on this and other libraries is given later in the chapter.
- *Current information is the best.* For really up-to-date information, look at the relevant periodical.

Many magazines have an index to previous articles on the inside back page, or will send you a full bibliography on request.

If you don't know which publications to consult, look at the British Humanities Index produced quarterly by the British Library Information Sciences Service. This book, which should be available at your reference library, gives an index by subject matter on UK publications for the previous three months. With the publication name and date you can obtain a back copy from the Back Numbers Department direct, or see if your reference library holds a copy. Many local libraries will obtain photocopies of articles from the comprehensive publications stocks held by the British Library in London – but this obviously takes time.

Newspapers can be an excellent source of current information but it helps to know what you're looking for. In those instances you can obtain a back copy from the newspaper direct, or see if the newspaper is stocked at your local library. Alternatively, you can consult the Official Publications and Social Sciences Service at the British Library which holds stocks of *The Times*, *Financial Times* and *International Herald Tribune* for the preceding month. The newspaper library at Colindale (also part of the British Library) has a comprehensive stock of newspaper back copies but also maintains current files on the *Observer*, *The Times* and *Sunday Times*. For more details about these libraries, see pages 113–118.

If you'd like to find out what has appeared in newspapers on a particular subject, consult *Keesing's Contemporary Archives* at your reference library. This gives a synopsis and index of current news and subjects.

The only British daily newspaper to be indexed is *The Times*. The first index appeared in 1790. Since 1973, the *Sunday Times* has been in the monthly index which has an annual cumulation. The only other newspaper to be indexed is the *New York Times*.

## Information sources

● The *Information Bureau* is for the use of the general public (although most of its callers are in fact businesses) and is open as a telephone service from Monday to Friday 9.30 am to 5.30 pm. The service was previously run by the *Daily Telegraph* but became independent in November 1990 and is now less restrictive in the kind of information supplied.

Jane Hall, one of the partners of the Bureau, told me that it receives infinitely varied questions about sport (facts and fixtures), etiquette, geography, history (ancient and modern), current affairs, company information, events and anniversaries, general information, tourist information and legal, medical, financial and technical matters. It also receives a lot of questions from secretaries doing research for their bosses!

Most questions are answered while the caller waits; those requiring more detailed research are supplied by telephone or fax later in the day. In order to be able to supply the information required, reference books are kept up to date recording deaths, major appointments and important changes in government, finance, business etc. The Bureau also accesses several on-line databases.

A subscription service costs £40 per hour and *ad hoc* information costs £5 for five minutes (or £60 per hour when extensive research is required). Payment is by Access/Visa but the Bureau is prepared to invoice business users. Contact: The Information Bureau, 51 Battersea Business Centre, 103 Lavender Hill, London SW11 5QL; tel 071-924 4414; fax 071-924 4456.

- *Company information.* All registered companies have to submit financial details on a regular basis to their particular registration authority.

Searches of records registered in England and Wales can be carried out at the following locations:

Companies Registration Office, Crown Way, Maindy, Cardiff CF4 3UZ; tel 0222 380801/380124 – open Monday to Friday 9.30 am to 4.00 pm

London Search Room, Companies House, 55–71 City Road, London EC1Y 1BB; 071-253 9393 – open Monday to Friday 9.45 am to 4.00 pm

Companies House – Birmingham, Birmingham Public Library, Chamberlain Square, Birmingham B3 3HQ; tel 021-233 9047

Companies House – Leeds, 25 Queen Street, Leeds LS1 2TW; tel 0532 338338

Companies House – Manchester, 75 Mosley Street, Manchester M2 2HR; tel 061-838 5080

Searches for company information for Scottish registered companies can be carried out at: Companies Registration Office, 102 George Street, Edinburgh EH2 3DJ; tel 031-225 5774 and Companies House – Glasgow, 21 Bothwell Street, Glasgow G6 6NR; tel 041-248 3315

Northern Ireland operates its own independent Companies Act

and enquiries about companies registered there should be addressed to: Registrar of Companies, Department of Commerce, 43–47 Chichester Street, Belfast BT1 4RJ; tel 0232 34121/4.

The search facilities in London, Cardiff and Edinburgh are based on microfilm records of original company documents. Details of all live companies are held, together with those dissolved since 1976. Scottish records can be ordered in Cardiff and London, and records for England and Wales from Edinburgh. The search fee is currently £2.75 per company (£20 for the 20-minute premium service search), and photocopies of fiche information are charged extra (10p per page). A same-day courier delivery service is available for central London (£15 per search including delivery).

Copies of company information can be obtained by post, in the form of either microfiche or photocopies. Charges are (1991):

£5, including postage, for a microfiche of each company record. An additional charge may be made for long lists of shareholders held on separate roll films;

£6.50 for a photocopy of an annual return, annual accounts, or the latest notification of registered office address delivered by a company;

Certificated copies of documents and certificates of fact can be obtained for £11.

Various other facilities are available including facsimile search, archive search, current directory and index of incorporated companies, new companies, dissolved companies etc. Orders may be placed by telephoning 0222 380124 (premium service), 0222 380411 (postal search), 0222 380336 (archive search), 0222 380 554 (courier delivery service), 0222 380 554 (facsimile search) and 0222 380124 (directory services).

The Department of Trade and Industry produces a number of useful leaflets which give more detailed information on the above, and are available free of charge from Cardiff.

- *Extel cards.* Extel Financial Ltd produces a range of card services giving financial information on over 8000 companies worldwide. All cards have a standard format and give regularly updated details of:

— Directors;
— Balance sheets;
— Activities;
— Ownership and subsidiaries;
— Capitalisation data;

— Profit and loss accounts;
— Chairman's statement;
— Recent news.

Extel cards are provided on a subscription basis with regular updates. For details contact: Customer Services Centre, Extel Financial Ltd, Fitzroy House, 13–17 Epworth Street, London EC2A 4DL; tel 071-251 3333; telex 884319; fax 071-251 2725.
Alternatively, many public libraries stock the cards.

- *The Financial Times Business Research Centre (BRC)* is a business information subscription service tailor-made to meet client specifications. The BRC can provide company information and Extel cards, market reports and surveys, statistics and biographical information. In-depth reports can be compiled to meet individual client requirements. The team of 20 researchers use business publications, on-line databases, professional contacts and the resources of the *Financial Times* library.

Subscriptions cost £500 per year, with an initial deposit of £295. *Ad hoc* research is also undertaken and charged at £95 per research hour. For full details contact: Tim Burchinall, Financial Times Business Research Centre, 1 Southwark Bridge, London SE1 9HL; tel 071-873 4102.

- If you are trying to see your way through official statistics, there is an excellent free publication to help you. This is 'Government Statistics: a Brief Guide to Sources', which is updated annually and available from: Central Statistical Office, Government Offices, Great George Street, London SW1P 3AQ.

The Business Statistics Office also provides information on all enquiries concerning government statistics generally. Contact the Central Statistics Office, Government Buildings, Cardiff Road, Newport NP9 1XG; tel 0633 812973.

- Her Majesty's Stationery Office produces an annual catalogue which lists many HMSO books and publications by subject. This is obtainable free from HMSO Books, Publicity, Room 2C04, St Crispins, Duke Street, Norwich NR3 1PD; tel 0603 694497. A full list of all HMSO publications can be obtained by purchasing or subscribing to their annual and monthly catalogues. Details from: PC51D, HMSO Books, PO Box 276, London SW8 5DT; tel 071-873 9090 (orders) or tel 071-873 0011 (enquiries).

- Conversely, the Department of Trade and Industry (DTI) produces a list of documents *not* sold by HMSO but issued by:

— Department of Trade and Industry;
— Department of Energy;

109

— The Monopolies and Mergers Commission;
— Office of Fair Trading;
— Office of Gas Supply;
— Office of Telecommunications.

This booklet issued annually is called 'Publications '90: a list of documents not sold by HMSO' and is available free of charge from: Department of Trade and Industry, Library and Information Centre, Room LG09, 1–19 Victoria Street, London SW1H 0ET; fax 071 215 5665.

The DTI also produces a catalogue detailing export-related publications indexed by country and product sector. This can be obtained free from: DTI Export Publications, PO Box 55, Stratford-Upon-Avon, Warwick CV37 9GE; tel 0789 296212.

● *Single European Market.* Both HMSO and the DTI have made special provision for providing information on the SEM.

HMSO has joined the fax revolution to help UK firms get their hands on vital European Community information quickly. Anyone with a fax machine can now have:

● actual/proposed legislation;
● tender opportunities;
● European Parliament decisions;
● reports from the European Court of Justice;
● European Commission working documents.

This information is retrieved almost instantly from HMSO's optical disc storage system and faxed directly. The system is called Scanfax and customers pay 50p per page (minimum £4). Businesses that already know what they want can order by phone (071-873 8220) or fax (071-873 8327). Alternatively, you can call the HMSO enquiry line (071-873 8327) for more guidance on what is available.

The DTI has set up a series of hotlines for people who require information about the SEM and the EC in general. For general enquiries about the SEM ring 081-200 1992. For specific questions the hotline will put you in touch with the DTI or other experts on the Single Market programme. A multitude of publications on the SEM are available from the DTI (see their annual publications guide above) and can be ordered using their 1992 hotline.

## Useful reference books

If you are at a complete loss where to look for the information you need, then consult:

- *Guide to Reference Material* by A J Walford, published by the British Library in three volumes:

  Vol 1 – Science and technology;
  Vol 2 – Social and historical sciences, philosophy and religion
  Vol 3 – Generalia, language, the arts and literature.

  In all, there are over 17,000 entries giving a comprehensive bibliography of reference material.

Alternatively, you may like to look at the abridged version of the above (only 2500 entries): *Walford's Concise Guide to Reference Material* by A J Walford, published by the British Library.

Another useful 'book of books' is:

*Top 3000 Directories and Annuals*, edited by M Rosdall and published by Alan Armstrong and Associates.

## General commerce

- Dun and Bradstreet's *Key British Enterprises* (Britain's top 20,000 companies)
- *Guide to World Commodity Markets* (Kogan Page)
- *Kompass Register of UK and Commercial Companies* (by country)
- *Stock Exchange Official Yearbook* (Macmillan) – official reference book giving authoritative information about what is bought and sold on the Stock Exchange.
- *Who Owns Whom* (Dun and Bradstreet) – a directory of parent, associate and subsidiary companies published annually.

## Accountancy

- Association of Certified Accountants list of members (published by ACA)
- Institute of Chartered Accountants in England and Wales – list of members in practice and firms shown topographically (UK and rest of world)

## Advertising and PR

- *Advertisers' Annual* (published by IPC Business Press) gives advertising agencies and PR consultants with their current clients. Listings for professional artists, photographers and graphic designers.

## Charities

- *Directory of Charities* (published by the Charities Aid Foundation)

(1989) gives comprehensive descriptions of charities in alphabetical order.

- *International Foundation Directory* (published by Europa Publications) gives international foundations, trusts and non-profit making institutions by country.

## Education

- *The Education Authorities Directory and Annual* (published annually by School Government Publishing Co).

## Health service

- *Hospitals & Health Service Yearbook and Directory of Hospital Suppliers* (published by the Institute of Health Services Management gives hospitals and health authorities by region.

## Management consultancy

- *Britain's Management Consultancy Industry* (vol 1: Large companies; vol 2: Small companies) (published by Jordan Information Services).

## People

- *Who's Who* gives biographical information about eminent people in the UK (published annually by A & C Black).
- *International Who's Who* (published by Europa Publications) gives biographical information about eminent people in all countries.

## Personnel

- *The Human Resource Management Yearbook 1990–91*, Consultant editor Michael Armstrong (published by Kogan Page) is a handbook for personnel and training managers.

## Press

- *British Rate and Data* (Maclean-Hunter, monthly).
- *Willing's Press Guide* (Thomas Skinner Directories).

## Qualifications

- *British Qualifications* (Kogan Page) lists all academic, technical, educational and professional qualifications available in Britain today. It also gives details of the relevant professional and trade bodies and information on membership.

## Travel

- *Travel Trade Directory* (published by Morgan-Grampian) gives travel and tour companies, airlines and travel trade information.

## Working abroad

- *Working Abroad: The Daily Telegraph Guide to Working and Living Overseas* by Godfrey Golzen (Kogan Page) gives useful information on the general aspects of working abroad, and has a country by country listing.

## Yearbooks

- *Whitaker's Almanack* (published annually by Whitaker) gives current information on people, organisations and events in the UK.
- *Statesman's Yearbook* (published annually by Macmillan) is a statistical and historical annual of the states of the world.
- *The Europa World Yearbook.* In two volumes gives detailed information on the political, economic and commercial institutions of the world.

## Special libraries

One of the most informative guidebooks to special libraries is *Guide to Libraries and Information Units in Government Departments and Other Organizations* produced regularly by the British Library. The 1990 edition (the 29th) has 99 pages of sensible information on all manner of specialist libraries and departments. The Guide is available in many reference libraries, but is also available direct from the Science Reference and Information Service (address on page 119) – price £30.

### National libraries

The following information is reproduced from *Guide to Libraries and Information Units* by kind permission of the British Library.

### The British Library

The British Library Board, 2 Sheraton Street,
London W1V 4BH; tel 071-323 7111
Central Administration
Press and Public Relations Section
   The British Library is the national library for the United Kingdom, formed in 1973 from several major national institutions. It is organised into two main operating Divisions: Humanities and Social Sciences and

Science, Technology and Industry, which also includes the Copyright Receipt Office, the National Bibliographic Service (NBS) and BLAISE, the British Library Automated Information Service.

*Humanities and Social Sciences*
Great Russell Street, London WC1B 3DG
tel 071-636 1544

PUBLIC SERVICES

Contains printed books and periodicals on humanities and social sciences. Apart from the general library it also comprises the Official Publications Library, the Newspaper Library and the former Library Association Library, now known as the British Library Information Sciences Service. The collections now contain over 9 million books and periodicals. (NB. Because of lack of space about 50 per cent of the stock has to be outhoused and items take up to 24 hours to be delivered.)

Reading Room, Bloomsbury
(address as above)
For reference and research which cannot readily be done elsewhere. Application must be made in person or by letter and proof of identity is needed. Telephone calls from intending users are welcome. A leaflet 'Applying for a Reader's Pass' is available.

Admissions and General Enquiries: 071-323 7677/7678 Reference help and bibliographic advice are given by post and telephone on all subjects covered in the main library and on specialist materials as indicated below. A full photographic and reprographic service is provided. The division is closed on Sundays, Good Friday, Christmas Eve, Bank Holidays, and for the week following the last complete week in October.
Hours: 09.00–17.00 Monday, Friday, Saturday, 09.00–21.00 Tuesday, Wednesday, Thursday.

Official Publications and Social Sciences Service
Provides reference and bibliographical enquiry services for the Reference Division's collection of current and historical government publications of all countries, for the publications of inter-governmental bodies such as the League of Nations, the United Nations and the European Communities, and for social science subjects. The OP and SS Reading Room houses an open access collection of up-to-date reference works in the social sciences including a selection of reference books and loose-leaf services on law; bibliographies of official publications; House of Commons Sessional Papers from 1715; UK legislation (including Local and Personal Acts); Journals and Debates of both Houses of Parliament;

current UK electoral registers; and, among other current information sources, the full range of press notices from UK government departments and the latest European Communities documents. Telephone enquiries are welcome, and there is a direct telephone link to OP & SS from the Business Information Service of the Science Reference and Information Service which OP & SS supports by answering enquiries concerned with business law or statistical information not held in SRIS. OP & SS has access to several on-line information services, which are used when appropriate in answering enquiries.
Enquiries: 071-323 7536.
Hours: 09.30–16.45 Monday, Friday, Saturday; 09.30–20.45 Tuesday, Wednesday, Thursday

Newspaper Library
Colindale Avenue, London NW9 5HE; tel 071-636 7357
  Holds London newspapers from 1801 onward; English provincial, Scottish, Irish, Commonwealth and foreign newspapers from about 1700 onward. Also holds many weekly and larger sized periodicals. (*The London Gazette* and all London newspapers published before 1801 are kept at Great Russell Street.) Admission by pass issued either at Colindale (for the Newspaper Library only) or in the main building, Great Russell Street (see above). Total holdings: 570,000 volumes and parcels, 220,000 microfilm reels; 3,000 current titles.
Enquiries: *Reading Room enquiries* ext 7353/7377: general enquiries, conditions of admission, etc. *Information Officer* ext 7357: detailed enquiries about newspapers, cataloguing queries, foreign language material, arrangements for visits. *Photographic Office* ext 7355: microfilm estimates and invoices, general photographic queries.
Hours: 10.00–16.45 Monday to Saturday. Last issue of newspapers 16.15.

British Library Information Sciences Service (BLISS)
7 Ridgmount Street, London WC1E 7AE; 071-323 7688; telex 21897
Stock: British and foreign books and pamphlets (approximately 86,000), and periodicals (approximately 1,250 current titles) on librarianship, information science and related subjects such as the book trade. Microforms and some audio-visual material are also held. Special collections: theses on librarianship.
Availability: Reference use is available to all; borrowing is restricted to Library Association members, British Library staff and applications on British Library Document Supply Centre loan forms.
Hours: 09.00–18.00 Monday, Wednesday, Friday; 09.00–20.00 Tuesday and Thursday, except mid-July to mid-September, when the hours are 09.00–18.00 Monday to Friday.

Services: Enquiry service available. Loans, subject to restrictions noted above. Photocopying.

## SPECIAL COLLECTIONS

### Manuscripts

Great Russell Street, London WC1B 3DG; tel 071-323 7500; telex 21462

An extensive collection of manuscripts (approximately 85,000 volumes), including books and documents of all kinds, in all European languages, ranging from Greek papyri to modern material. Charters and rolls, detached seals, manuscript music, maps, plans, topographical drawings, and many literary and historical autographs are included. Facilities to readers are provided in a Students' Room for which a pass is required. The Department provides a full range of information and photographic services. The Department is closed on Sundays, Good Friday, Christmas Eve, Christmas Day, Boxing Day, New Year's Day, May Day and the week after that during which the Printed Books Reading Room is closed (normally the Manuscripts Room closure will fall in the second week in November).

### Map Library

Enquiries: tel 071-323 7700/7703

The map collection comprises about 1,600,000 items including atlases, maps, charts and globes as well as topographical views in both manuscript and printed form. In particular the collection covers British cartography past and present, the Ordnance Survey of Great Britain, Colonial and Revolutionary maps of America, Renaissance cartography and thematic maps. The special collections are King George III's Topographical Collection, King George III's Maritime Collection, the Crace Collection of maps and plans of London, the Beudeker Collection of Dutch maps and views (1600–1750). The Map Library also holds current topographic maps series for all parts of the world at scales 1:50,000 and smaller. An archive of Landsat imagery of the British Isles is held with catalogues and browse film of satellite imagery for all areas of the world.

Hours: 09.00–16.30 Monday to Saturday (09.30 with reader's pass). Access by readers pass or by day pass on production of signed identification.

Enquiry service by correspondence, personal visit and telephone.

### Music Library

An extensive collection of British and foreign printed music. Special collections include the Royal Music Library noted for its Handel autographs and the Paul Hirsch Music Library.

Enquiries: tel 071-323 7528

Hours: *Music Reading Area:* as for Official Publications Library; *Music Library:* 09.30–16.30 Monday to Friday.

Philatelic Collections
Great Russell Street, London WC1E 3DG and 14 Shore Street, London WC1E 7DG; tel 071-323 7635; telex 21462
  Comprises 25 major and a number of smaller collections containing approximately 6 million items.
Hours: All material not on public display is available by appointment from Monday to Friday (except Public Holidays) from 10.00–16.00.

Oriental Collections
14 Store Street, London WC1E 7DG; tel 071-636 1544; telex 21462
  The collection includes 614,000 printed volumes (including bound serials and newspapers) and 41,390 volumes of manuscripts in, and concerning, the languages and cultures of North Africa, the Near and Middle East, and the whole of Asia. It is particularly rich in Hebrew, Arabic, Turkish, Persian, Indian and Chinese manuscripts, and there are important collections of Chinese, Japanese and Tibetan block-printed books. Contemporary material on the countries and peoples of Asia is also well represented; attention is also being given to official and governmental publications. Facilities for readers are provided in the Oriental Reading Room for which a pass is required. A full range of photographic and information services is provided. The section's publications include catalogues and a guide to the collections. The section is closed on Sundays, Good Friday, Christmas Eve, Christmas Day, Boxing Day, and the week preceding the last complete week in October.
Enquiries: Ext 7642 (Reading Room), 7660 (Administration).
Hours: 09.30–17.00 Monday to Friday; 09.30–13.00 Saturday.

India Office Library and Records
197 Blackfriars Road, London SE1 8NG; tel 071-928 9531
Services: Mainly for reference but some books can be borrowed by other libraries and registered readers. Microfilm, photostat and xerox facilities.
Availability: Open to the general public for reference purposes. Membership (with tickets) required for longer-term use and for loans.
Hours: Main Reading Room (197 Blackfriars Road) 09.30–18.00 Monday to Friday; 09.30–13.00 Saturday.

National Sound Archive
29 Exhibition Road, London SW7 2AS; tel 071-589 6603
  Stock and subject coverage: The Archive holds nearly half a million discs and over 55,000 hours of recorded tape. It aims to be comprehen-

sive with special responsibility to British recording. Includes popular music of all kinds, oral history, sound effects and documentary material, with special collections of western art music, international music, wildlife sounds, drama and spoken literature, selective recordings from BBC broadcasts, BBC transcription discs and duplicate copies of BBC Sound Archives material. Through voluntary deposit it attempts to acquire one copy of each disc commercially issued in the UK, makes its own recordings at outside venues and encourages deposit of private collections. The library contains printed material, microfilm and microfiche relating to sound recordings, eg catalogues, discographies, periodicals and reference works.

Availability: To any member of the public. No reader's pass or appointment necessary for the library: listening service by appointment, except for demonstration cassettes introducing the Archive, which can usually be heard without appointment.

Hours: *Library:* 09.30–16.30 Monday to Friday, late opening to 21.00 Thursday. *Listening service:* (by appointment) 09.30–16.30 Monday to Friday, late opening to 21.00 Thursday.

*Northern listening service:* at British Library Document Supply Centre, Boston Spa, West Yorkshire LS23 7BQ; tel 0937 843434 Hours: 09.15–16.30 Monday to Friday.

Services: Free listening service; information service; transcription service; lectures on artistic, technical and scientific aspects of sound recordings. Further information about any services available by post, telephone or personal visit.


*Science, Technology and Industry*
British Library
Document Supply Centre,
Boston Spa, Wetherby, West Yorkshire LS23 7BQ; tel 0937 843434; telex 557381; fax 0937 546333 CCITT (Group 1)
A document supply service covering all subject fields and providing a rapid loan and photocopy service to organisations throughout the world. There is a public reading room.

Stock: About 7 million items including: 56,000 different serial titles covering all subjects in all languages; 500,000 translations into English, mainly from Russian scientific and technical serials; 2,800,000 monographs; over 2 million unclassified technical reports mainly of US origin; 500,000 doctoral theses; 111,000 music scores and 250,000 conference proceedings.

Loans: To registered customers using the printed, prepaid requisition forms.

Document copying: Microfilm and xerographic copies produced.
Other services: Urgent Action Service: Medical Information Service.

Science Reference and Information Service (SRIS)
The Science Reference and Information Service is the national library
for modern science, technology and commerce including patents, trade
marks and designs. It has the most comprehensive reference collection in
Western Europe of such literature from the whole world. The Library's
primary purpose is to make information from its wealth of literature
readily accessible to research and development scientists, technologists
and engineers, to industry and to those who work on their behalf. Its
facilities are thus available to information officers, researchers, abstrac-
tors, technical journalists, industrial managers, librarians, patent and
trade mark agents. It is open to any adult member of the public, and no
reader's pass is required. An enquiry service is available for those who
cannot visit the library in person. There are special services providing
business information, Japanese information and on-line searching of
computerised databases; photocopying and linguistic help are also
available. A charge is made for some services: further details on request.
Stock: Serials: over 60,000; Abstracting serials: 1400; Monographs:
approximately 200,000; Patent specifications: approximately 29 million;
Dictionaries and glossaries; Trade directories: 2000; Market surveys:
2500; Trade literature, company information.

Reading Rooms
(i) 25 Southampton Buildings, Chancery Lane, London WC2A 1AW;
071-323 7494; Electronic mail BL1404; telex 266959; fax 071-323 7930
Enquiries: General, ext 7494; British and EPO Patents, ext 7919;
Foreign Patents, 7902; Business Information Service ext 7457; Biotech-
nology information ext 7293; Japanese information ext 7924; On-line
Search Centre ext 7477.
Subject coverage: Physical sciences and technologies, engineering,
business information, patents and patent literature.
Hours: *Main Reading Room*, 09.30–21.00 Monday to Friday; 10.00–13.00
Saturday. *Foreign Patents Reading Room* (in Chancery House) 09.30–17.30
Monday to Friday.
(ii) 9 Kean Street, London WC2B 4AT; tel 071-323 7288
Subject coverage: Life sciences and technologies, medicine, agriculture,
earth sciences and mathematics.
Hours: 09.30–17.30 Monday to Friday.

**National Library of Scotland**
George IV Bridge, Edinburgh EH1 1EW; tel 031-226 4531; telex 72638
NLSEDIG; fax 031-225 9944/031-226 5620

Stock and subject coverage: 5 million volumes and pamphlets. Under copyright legislation the Library receives all British and Irish publications, including all Stationery Office publications, all Parliamentary Papers, a proportion of departmental publications of the United Nations and other international bodies sold by HMSO. A large selection of USA government publications is received by exchange. Depository library for publications of WHO, ICAO and ICJ. Foreign and antiquarian books purchased extensively. 16,500 current periodicals. 230 newspapers, mostly Scottish, main English national, technical and a few foreign. In addition to the main collection of the old Advocates' Library, there are many special collections, including Incunabula, early Scottish books, English plays, Spanish, Scandinavian, Scottish Gaelic, Alpine, Polar, Baking, Jacobite, Phrenology, Liturgies, Theology, Children's Books.

*Maps:* Copyright collection, including Ordnance Survey maps from the earliest issues and Scottish maps of all periods.

*Music:* Copyright collection, and special collections of Scottish and English music, Berlioz, Handel and Verdi.

*Manuscripts:* Gaelic, Icelandic, medieval archives of families and institutions (mainly Scottish); drawings, maps and plans; papers of important Scottish men of affairs and letters.

*Scottish Science Library:* Incorporates the Scottish Business Information Service and holds a wide range of business and technical material on open access. 33 Salisbury Place, Edinburgh EH9 1SL; tel 031-226 4531.

Availability: Reading Rooms and Map Room open for reference and research not easily carried out elsewhere. Tickets on application.

Loans: See following entry.

Hours: 09.30–20.30 Monday to Friday; 09.30–13.00 Saturday. The Map Room closes at 17.00 Monday–Friday throughout the year. The Scottish Science Library is open 09.30–17.00 Monday, Tuesday, Thursday and Friday; 09.30–20.30 on Wednesday. Library closed Christmas Day, Boxing Day, New Year's Day and the day following, the first Monday in May and Good Friday.

Other services: Photographic reproduction, microfilm and Xerox, beta radiography, plan variograph.

*Lending Services*

Causewayside Building, 33 Salisbury Place, Edinburgh EH9 1SL; tel 031-226 4531; telex 72638 NLSEDIG: fax 031-226 5620

Holds a stock of approx 120,000 vols. Headquarters for interlending between all Scottish public and non-public libraries. Enquiries and inter-library loan applications should be addressed to the Superintendent of Lending Services. A *Scottish Union Catalogue*, with at present approximately 2 million entries, is in compilation.

## National Library of Wales

Aberystwyth, Dyfed SY23 3BU; tel 0970 623816; telex 35165; fax 0970 615709

Stock and subject coverage: A legal deposit library since 1912 for UK and Irish publications with over 3 million books including government and Welsh local authority publications and a large collection of periodicals, newspapers, maps and manuscripts. Foreign books, mainly in humanities, are acquired by purchase or exchange. Special interest is in all material (MSS, books, periodicals, maps, graphic material and audio-visual) relating to Wales and other Celtic countries. Deposit library for UN, UNESCO, WHO and other international governmental agencies.

*Maps:* Copyright collections; Welsh tithe maps and apportionments; topographical prints and drawings.

*Manuscripts:* Special collections of Welsh manuscripts and of records relating to Wales; Welsh Probate Records to 1857; Records of the Church in Wales; Quarter Sessions Records for Cardigan, Montgomery, Brecon and Radnor; Records of the Courts of Great Sessions, 1542-1830; papers of modern politicians and literary figures.

Availability: Reading Room and Map Room open for reference and research to holders of readers' tickets.

Hours: 09.30-18.00 Monday to Friday; 09.30-17.00 Saturday and general holidays. Closed on Sundays; Good Friday to Easter Tuesday inclusive; May Day, Spring Bank Holiday, August Bank Holiday, first full week in October, Christmas Day, Boxing Day and one other day; New Year's Day.

Other services: Xerox and microfilm facilities. Headquarters of the Regional Libraries Bureau for Wales. Enquiry service. Exhibitions.

## Economics and finance

### Confederation of British Industry

Centre Point, 103 New Oxford Street, London WC1A 1DU; tel 071-379 7400; telex 21332; fax 071-240 1578

Enquiries: Ext 2729

Subject coverage: Industry and government relations, economic policy, parliamentary affairs, statistics, industrial relations, wages and conditions of employment, industrial and company law, energy and natural resources policy, education and training, technology policy, European and wider international aspects of industrial policy.

Archives: CBI's predecessor organisations to 1965; papers held on permanent loan by the Modern Records Centre, University of Warwick Library, Coventry CV4 7AL; tel 0203 523523 ext 2014

121

Availability: To members but also co-operating libraries and others by arrangement.
Hours: 09.30–17.30 Monday to Friday.
Services: Enquiries, loans, photocopies, microfilm reader/printer, on-line service, fax.

## Labour, work employment

### Employment Department
HQ Library, Steel House, Tothill Street, London SW1H 9NF; tel 071-273 followed by appropriate extension.
Librarian: K Bradbury, FLA; Ext 4707
Deputy Librarian: D Aitchison; Ext 4708
Library enquiries: (Books) Exts 4711/4714; (Periodicals) Ext 4710; (Translations) Ext 4722
Stock and subject coverage: Totals over 100,000 volumes. All subjects within the Department's range are well represented, eg industrial relations, trade unions, working conditions, management, employment, wages, racial discrimination, women's employment.
Availability: For reference to bona fide research students. Notice to visit is required.
Hours: 09.00–17.00 Monday to Friday.
Services: Enquiry service; loans to other libraries; photocopies.

### Work Research Unit Information System (ACAS)
Room 111, 27 Wilton Street, London SW1X 7AZ; tel 071-210 3895
Stock and subject coverage: Approximately 17,000 items, mainly pamphlets, articles and cuttings. 100 books and 200 journals scanned. Covers job satisfaction, motivation, job redesign, the quality of working life, industrial psychology, industrial sociology, job enrichment, job enlargement, new ways of working, micro-processors, effects of new technology and management of change.
Availability and services: The Unit aims to promote improvements in the quality of working life; the Information System, as a publicity and reference organisation, is available to all on request. Enquiries by letter or telephone and visits to scan the files can be arranged with the librarian.

### Employment Department Library
Room E354, Moorfoot, Sheffield S1 4PQ; tel 0742 753275
Stock and subject coverage: Approximately 15,000 items and 300 current periodicals, mainly post-1974. Subjects covered include man-power planning, employment services, training psychology, vocational education, youth unemployment etc. Fairly complete collection of

publications by industrial training boards.
Availability: For reference to bona fide research students. Prior notice of intention to visit is requested.
Loans: To other government departments and reciprocating libraries. Telephone requests to 0742 753275.
Hours: 09.00–17.00 Monday to Friday.
Services: Enquiry service; loans (as above); photocopies, microfiche reading/copying facilities.

## Public administration

### Scottish Office Library Services

(HQ) New St Andrews House, Edinburgh EH1 3TG; tel 031-556 8400; telex 727301
The various libraries serve: the Department of Agriculture and Fisheries for Scotland, Scottish Development Department; Scottish Education Department; Scottish Home and Health Department.
Stock: Approximately 100,000 books and pamphlets; 2,000 current periodical titles.
Availability: To staff of the Department; members of the public admitted by appointment for reference use only.
Hours: 08.30–17.00 Monday to Thursday; 08.30–16.30 Friday.
Services: Enquiry service; loans to other libraries; photocopies; newspaper cuttings; sale of Scottish Office publications.

New St Andrews House Library
Edinburgh EH1 3TG; tel 031-556 8400
Subject coverage: Scottish administration, economics, education, law, physical planning, transport.

St Andrews House Library
Edinburgh EH1 3TG; tel 031-556 8400
Subject coverage: Public health, social work, architecture, criminal justice, housing, prison service.

Agricultural Scientific Services Station Library
East Craigs, Edinburgh EH12 8NJ; tel 031-339 8400
Subject coverage: Seed testing, plant diseases, nematology, crop entomology, control of pests, wild life control.

### Welsh Office Library

Cathays Park, Cardiff CF1 3NQ; tel 0222 825111; telex 49228
Enquiries, loans: All subjects except agriculture, Cathays Park, ext 3362
Stock and subject coverage: Approximately 50,000 volumes and pamphlets on administration in Wales covering industry, planning,

roads, health services, local government, education and agriculture. 1000 current periodicals taken.

Availability: To the general public for reference only by appointment.

Hours: 09.00–17.00 Monday to Friday.

Services: Enquiry service; photocopies; loans to Welsh Office staff, other government departments and inter-library loans to all other libraries.

Welsh Office Agriculture Department Library
Trawsgoed, nr Aberystwyth, Dyfed SY23 4HT;
tel 097 43 301 ext 206/264
Subject coverage: Agriculture.
Availability: as above.
Hours: 08.30–16.30 Monday to Friday.

## Press cutting agencies and picture libraries

If you need to use the services of the above, consult the *Writers' and Artists' Yearbook* (published annually by A & C Black) which has several pages of entries under these categories. The book should be in your local reference library.

## Weird and wonderful

How do you go about finding unusual goods and services which may occasionally be needed during the course of your job (eg the colostomy bags mentioned in the Introduction)? First, assume the mantle of a detective and use your imagination. Second, always let your fingers do the walking.

Where can you begin looking for what is required?

- Consult the Yellow Pages or Business Pages directory for a large city. Even if your requirements aren't listed precisely, it can start off your enquiries. Ask organisations, similar to the one you're seeking, exactly where you can look. People are usually very helpful if you ask questions nicely.
- Look at the classified sections of weekend newspapers – they are positively bulging with advertisements for all manner of things.
- Contact the relevant trade association who should be able to steer you in the right direction.
- Get hold of the appropriate trade magazine which will probably have classified advertisements.

This is a very small selection of the kinds of goods and services which it is possible to track down using some of the methods mentioned. However, the listing does not necessarily imply recommendation.

# For the office

- *Typing head alterations.* New characters/symbols/logos can be inserted on your own typesphere/printwheel. Contact:

  Mrs Linda Messider, Typesphere/Printwheel Division, Butler & Tanner Ltd, Selwood Printing Works, Frome, Somerset BA11 1NF; tel 0373 51500.

- *Rubber stamps.* Can be produced to your own specification. Contact:

  Mark C Brown & Son Ltd, PO Box 69, 4 Baker Street, Hull HU2 8HS; tel 0482 23464.

  Prontaprint branches.

- *Crate hire for removals.* Contact:

  GB Crate Hire Ltd, Unit 9, Cranford Way, Tottenham Lane, Hornsey, London N8 9DG; 081-340 9535.

- *Commercial air cleaners.* Contact:

  Trion Ltd, West Portway Industrial Estate, Andover, Hants SP10 3SL; tel 0264 64622.

# Gift tokens

- *National garden gift tokens.* Can be bought/exchanged at most garden centres, or send SAE to:

  The Horticulture Trades Association, 19 High Street, Theale, Reading, Berkshire; tel 0734 302092.

- *West End theatre tokens.* Available in £1, £5, £10 and £20 units from most West End theatres, or by post from:

  Tokens, Society of West End Theatres, Bedford Chambers, Covent Garden Piazza, London WC2E 8HQ; tel 071-836 0971.

- *Wine gift tokens.* Available/exchangeable at Victoria Wine Stores and direct from:

  Direct Marketing Department, Victoria Wine Company, Brook House, Chertsey Road, Woking, Surrey GU21 5BE; tel 0483 715066.

125

## Food

- *Cheese Club*. Monthly cheese selection and newsletter.

  Paxton & Whitfield Ltd, 93 Jermyn Street, London SW1Y 6JE; tel 071-930 0250.

- *Smoked salmon by post*

  Clearwater Products, Ludbridge Mill, East Hendred, Wantage, Oxon OX12 8LN; tel 0235 833732.

## Health

- *24-hour private nursing care*

  British Nursing Association, North Place, 82 Great North Road, Hatfield, Herts AL9 5BL; tel 07072 63544.

- *Back pain products*

  The Back Shop, 24 New Cavendish Street, London W1M 7LH; tel 071-935 9120.

- *Home lifts*

  Stannah Lifts (Domestic Products) Ltd, Watt Close, East Portway, Andover, Hants SP10 3SD; tel 0264 64311.

## Flowers

- *Plants and flowers by post*

  Cornish Bulb Company, Little Greystones Farm, Passage Hill, Mylor, Falmouth, Cornwall; tel 0326 72720.

## Miscellaneous

- *Fireworks*

  Bracknell Fireworks Ltd, 2 Bullbrook Row, Bracknell, Berks RG12 2NL; tel 0344 425321.

- *Kites*

  Malvern Kites, Unicorn Yard, Great Malvern, Worcestershire WR14 4PZ; tel 06845 65504.

# Chapter 8

# How to Keep Smiling

## Surviving Christmas

Christmas is usually the busiest time of the office year and particularly so for secretaries who have to organise all that it entails. The secret of coping with this frantic time is to plan ahead.

### Christmas cards

It's never too soon to think about Christmas cards. Posting dates, particularly overseas, seem to get earlier each year, so you should aim to have your cards ordered by October at the very latest.

If in a new job, you may have inherited a perfectly typed (or word processed) Christmas card list – or nothing at all. If starting from scratch, make a provisional list by going through the address book and including every name – you can always delete some later. Note down your boss's subordinates and personal staff – everyone from his deputy to the cleaner. If you have inherited a 'list of cards received' from the previous year, this may prompt additional names. (You may like to draw up one of these yourself for future reference depending, of course, on whether your boss is one of those people who thinks that received cards should be reciprocated.)

Discuss the draft with your boss and then prepare the final list. (Summer holiday time is a good opportunity for this.) If you are lucky enough to have a photocopier which transfers list addresses on to sheets of blank self-seal labels, you can save yourself some repetitious typing. Those with word processors are laughing of course! But even without these gadgets, you can manually type up rolls of self-seal address labels at any time in readiness for when the cards arrive.

Select your Christmas cards from the commercial and/or charity card catalogues which should be available from quality stationers or department stores. Many will deliver these to your office for a general inspection.

Decide how many cards are needed and order an extra two dozen – they'll always come in handy for next year (or for someone else who runs out). Place a written order with details of any overprinting required, eg your boss's and/or company name. Allow extra ordering time if you need this service.

When the cards arrive, put the pre-typed labels on the envelopes. If there are hundreds and you have plenty of time, give your boss a small batch of cards to sign each day with his post. Otherwise set aside a couple of signing hours in the diary.

Check with the Post Office on last posting dates and make sure you're ready in time. The receipt of Christmas cards at New Year smacks of inefficiency.

Keep a Christmas card for each year in your files to avoid duplication in the future – memories tend to be unreliable.

## Christmas gifts

About the beginning of December you might like to ask your boss (tactfully!) if he wishes to buy his staff Christmas presents, eg chauffeur, cleaner etc. If he does, this is a task which is almost bound to be relegated to you, so be prepared. Drinks, cosmetics, flowers or plants are all acceptable gifts but try to personalise yours by finding out the recipient's particular favourite. You should reap the benefit of this bit of Christmas spirit all year.

While you shouldn't assume the complete role of Santa Claus, it might be an idea for you to remind your boss diplomatically that he has a family to buy for. You could do this in a roundabout way by asking how his Christmas shopping plans are going. If he's organised – well and good. However, it's amazing how many pressurised executives fail to notice the onslaught of the festive season.

Should you buy your boss a Christmas present? Some people find this a difficult decision, particularly when working for someone new. It seems to be a general office tradition that most bosses buy their secretaries a small Christmas gift (or ask them to buy their own). Whether to return a gift or not is obviously a matter of personal choice. If you feel you'd like to, then pick something impersonal, eg something for the office or a bottle of wine. Alternatively, you could pick something really silly which will appeal to his sense of humour (assuming he has one, of course).

## The Christmas party

Organising the Christmas party is never the fun it sounds. However hard you try there will always be someone having a grumble about the arrangements. If faced with this unenviable task, what can you do to ensure its success?

Ask around (about September) and see what kind of party people prefer. If you have a mixed age group be prepared for a range of suggestions from a disco in the Chamber of Horrors to a formal meal in a restaurant. It is always difficult to strike the right balance but you'll probably have to settle on something 'safe' to suit the majority.

There is the very important question of cost. Whether the company or staff are paying for the party, you will have to budget carefully. Prices tend to be inflated at Christmas and you may find many options are out of financial reach (this gives you a cast iron excuse for those people with expensive tastes).

Do you have an evening or lunch-time function? An evening party is much less disruptive to office routine, but many people prefer a long lunch and short afternoon. If you do opt for an evening party, remember that most people will probably have to go home by public transport. If you are arranging something like a river cruise, make sure the boat docks before the last train leaves.

Once you have an idea of the kind of party, make arrangements early. Hotels and restaurants can get booked for the festive season in October.

If you have a choice, pick a party date as near to Christmas as possible. Even the best organised party can fall a bit flat if it occurs three weeks beforehand.

You may find that set menus are available if you decide on a meal. Circulate details of these and put in a written order well in advance. Remember to cater for any vegetarians. Most restaurants these days will prepare special meals if given sufficient warning. Obtain a wine list and have your in-house connoisseur make a selection (you then have someone else to blame if no one else approves!). Keep a record of the pre-selected food and drink as no one will remember what they have ordered so long in advance. Give everyone a reminder on the day itself.

Go along to the venue and place your order personally. See exactly where your party will sit and remember to discuss any extras, eg table decorations, flowers, crackers, Christmas trees. Follow up your visit with an itemised letter setting everything down in detail. You can't leave anything to chance at this busy season.

Remember to discuss the manner of payment. You may also need to pay a deposit for a large booking. Many establishments will send you a bill at a later date – but check this carefully.

Arrange for invitations to be printed (or word processed) and send these out in plenty of time. Keep a list of the people invited and check off their names as they reply.

Organise transport if necessary. A few days before the big event, send around final instructions which should give precise details about:

- Date and time;
- Venue;
- How to get there and whether transport is arranged;
- Central meeting point if applicable, eg for transport;
- Style of dress (if this is important);

- Approximate finishing time;
- Details of cost and method of payment (if applicable).

On the day before, ring the venue, transport service, and so on and check the final arrangements. After that, keep your fingers crossed!

## General

Finally, here are a few tips on surviving the general pre-Christmas rush:

- Allow for the uncertainty of postal deliveries and don't entrust anything urgent to the post;
- In the fortnight preceding Christmas, make important phone calls in the morning – other people have Christmas lunches too;
- Organise your private Christmas cards and gifts well in advance. When experiencing the pre-Christmas office rush, the last thing you'll feel like doing at lunch-time is trailing around overcrowded shops;
- Don't drink too much.

## Accidents and how to cope

Physical injury aside, life would be extremely boring if there wasn't the odd trivial mishap to keep us on our toes. The dictionary tells me that an accident is an 'event without apparent cause, or unexpected'. Haven't there been times in all our secretarial careers when we've come across our share of these?

How do you cope with an ordinary office accident (eg spilling coffee down a client, being locked in – or out), particularly if you were its inadvertent cause?

- *Keep calm.* There's no point in your adding to the general confusion by panicking. Take deep breaths if you have to.
- *Apologise politely* but not repeatedly. Accidents happen to us all.
- *Think logically and use your initiative* in taking steps to rectify the situation. Call in the experts if necessary, eg plumber, locksmith etc.
- *Keep smiling.* It's amazing how a bit of humour can improve a difficult situation.

While accidents obviously can't be totally avoided, they can teach us how to become more careful so they are less likely to occur. So don't despair if it happens to you – learn for the future.

Many offices have their own procedures for dealing with serious accidents but here are a few tips in case yours does not.

## Emergencies

- *If a colleague is taken seriously ill:*
  — Dial 999 if a real emergency;
  — Call in an emergency doctor (your local police station keeps lists of these, and emergency chemists too);
  — Call in your office first aid specialist;
  — Turn to the first aid notes below.

- *If you find a suspicious looking package (or one comes through the post):*
  — Don't touch it!
  — Get everyone out of the vicinity;
  — Call your security officer;
  — Dial 999 and ask for the police.

- *If you find a fire:*
  — Ring the fire bell and evacuate the building;
  — Dial 999 for the fire brigade.

- *If you come across a suspicious-looking stranger* (particularly if you work in a bank):
  — Make a few discreet enquiries by approaching the stranger and asking politely if you can help him;
  — If you're still worried, call in the security officer;
  — Ring the police.

## First aid notes

The following directions are reproduced by kind permission of the Order of St John:

### Artificial ventilation

If breathing has stopped, lay patient on his back, on a firm surface if possible, with head tilted back. Remove any foreign matter from mouth and pull chin forward to make a clear airway, checking that tongue is not blocking it. If patient is still not breathing, try mouth to mouth breathing.

To do this, open your mouth and take a deep breath. Pinch the patient's nostrils with your fingers, then seal his mouth with your lips (holding the head back all the time). Blow into the patient's mouth until the chest rises, then remove your mouth and watch his chest deflate. Repeat this as long as necessary at normal breath rate, but give the first four blows as rapidly as possible.

Once breathing starts place patient in recovery position (see *Unconsciousness*).

131

# Bleeding

To control heavy bleeding grasp the sides of the wound or press on it very firmly with a pad of the cleanest material available. If pad gets saturated apply another on top. A firm bandage can be used to secure the pad, but *never* use a tourniquet. To protect yourself from possible infection with HIV, wear rubber gloves or cover any cuts/open wounds of your own which might come into contact with the casualty's blood.

# Bone, broken or dislocated

Send for a doctor at once and do not touch or attempt to move limb (but it can be supported to prevent movement). Treat for shock if necessary.

# Burns and scalds

Cold water or other coolant should be applied in quantity to the burn or scald for at least 10 minutes or until the pain has ceased. Clothing need not be removed but exposed burns or scalds may be lightly covered by smooth clean material such as linen. No ointment or other similar material should be applied. Severely burned or scalded casualties should be taken to hospital as quickly as possible.

# Choking

Immediately bend the casualty over so that the head is lower than the lungs if possible. Strike three or four sharp blows between the shoulder blades. If the casualty loses consciousness open his mouth and with a crooked finger, try to find any obstruction and remove. Then give artificial ventilation (see *Artificial ventilation*).

# Fits

If someone falls to the ground with jerking movements this is probably an epileptic fit. Put something soft under his head (or cradle it in your hands), turning it to one side. Loosen tight clothing. *Never* force anything between the teeth and do not give anything to drink.

# Poisoning

If the casualty is conscious ask quickly what has happened as he may lapse into unconsciousness. Keep any container which may help to identify the poison.

If the lips and mouth show signs of burns give quantities of water or milk to dilute the poison. If the casualty is breathing freely, place him in the recovery position under observation. If breathing is failing, or has ceased, commence artificial respiration immediately. *In any case, take the casualty to hospital as quickly as possible.*

**Shock**

Even quite minor accidents sometimes cause shock. The patient should be lying down with head low and turned to one side, and legs raised a little (except in the case of head or chest injury). Cover lightly but do not heat. If conscious give sips of tepid water only.

**Unconsciousness**

If casualty is breathing put in *recovery position*, on his side with upper knee drawn up and head tilted back to keep airway open. Don't use a pillow. Send for doctor.

The above is only intended as a brief guide – more complex instructions (with diagrams) are to be found in the many excellent first aid books around. Two of these are:

> *Practical First Aid* produced by the British Red Cross Society in association with Dorling Kindersley;
> *First Aid Manual*, the authorised manual of St John Ambulance, St Andrew's Ambulance Association and the British Red Cross Society.

First aid courses are essential for us all. For details of those available near you, contact either St John's, St Andrew's or the Red Cross. Their numbers will be in the telephone directory.

## AIDS

AIDS (Acquired Immune Deficiency Syndrome) is a new and serious public health hazard throughout the world. At present it is important to prevent any further spread of infection by ensuring that people know how it is transmitted. Information about it is given in the booklet *AIDS and Employment*, prepared by the Department of Employment and the Health and Safety Executive, which is obtainable from: AIDS and Employment, The Mailing House, Leeland Road, London W13 9HL.

*Chapter 9*

# Information Technology:
# Friend or Foe?

Ten years ago the explosive growth of new technology in office environments made many people think that the 'paperless office' was just around the corner and office jobs would be seriously affected as a consequence. It is now clear that this is not the case. Despite the fact that almost all organisations now use computers and word processors, the impact on the number of jobs has been negligible and most offices still generate and deal with forests of paper!

Word processors are undoubtedly faster than typewriters but this has not caused a significant reduction in the number of secretaries. This is hardly surprising – the secretary's role is not one of simple text handling. However, new technology *has* altered the skill requirement of secretaries. Consider how IT can affect a common secretarial task – report production. Box 1 looks at the procedure adopted by the Managing Director's secretary in a traditional office.

---

Managing Director's Secretary
Company A: Traditional Office

- Telephone or write and mail individual memos to each sales department asking for figures.
- Use telephone and memos to chase up, coax and cajole when no response.
- Check through with departments whose figures seem incorrect.
- Chase up late information.
- Spend hours with calculator consolidating figures.
- Type report.
- Arrival of last-minute information changes whole picture, so . . .
- Recalculate figures.
- Retype report.
- Draw charts with ruler and pen – hope correcting fluid won't show when photocopied.
- Work late night before meeting to photocopy and collate reports.

The report is done but the secretary has spent most of the time on administrative trivia and rework, rather than the creative and productive side of the job.

---

**Box 1**

Compare this with the same role in a company using information technology.

---

Managing Director's Secretary
Company B: Electronic Office

- As report is typed on computer terminal, bring in figures electronically from each sales department's database of figures (entered at their own terminals as each sale was made).
- Figures are automatically consolidated by the program that the secretary uses.
- From the terminal's keyboard, use graphics capability of system to produce coloured charts on the screen – to show sales achievements against forecast, this month's figures against last month's, this year's against last year's – all from information already held in the system.
- Take in last-minute data and instruct system to recalculate totals and adjust charts accordingly.
- Instruct system to distribute report electronically to the terminal of each board member, to allow them time to print it out and read it before the meeting.
- Print out (ready collated) the Managing Director's copy, complete with neatly plotted charts.
- Move on to other work.

The final result is a highly professional report, quickly prepared, automatically filed in the system and easily retrievable whenever needed.

---

**Box 2**

Current predictions on the changing relationship between secretarial and managerial or professional roles suggest that secretaries will become more like PAs as their paper-handling role develops into a 'centre of competence'.

Newly qualified secretaries will be familiar with new technology but for those established in offices where new technology is only beginning to make an impact, or for women returning to a secretarial career after having a family, I shall try to throw a little light on a complex and somewhat confusing subject.

## General principles

Information technology is the application of microelectronics to traditional office routine. This can be expanded further by using the government's definition of information technology: 'the technology concerned with the acquisition, transmission, processing and presentation of information in all its forms – audio, visual, text and graphics.'

New technology is not therefore confined to text generation alone – whole data and communications processes can be transformed.

135

## Brief IT glossary

*Central processing unit.* The computer's 'brain' which controls its operation. It contains the arithmetic and logic unit, also the core memory.

*Daisywheel*, see *Printer*.

*Dot matrix*, see *Printer*.

*Floppy disk.* A flexible plastic or stiff metallic disk with a magnetic coating which allows text, data or programs to be stored. There is random access to text or data for editing purposes.

*Hardware.* All word processing/computer equipment, apart from the programs (software).

*Interface.* The connecting link between two systems, such as word processors/computers to peripherals, eg input, output and storage items.

*Laptop computer.* A small and highly portable personal computer increasingly used by executives on the move.

*Lazer*, see *Printer*.

*Printer.* A unit which produces output on paper (hard copy). The three main types are: *Daisywheel:* so called because the printwheel resembles a daisy with the characters on the tips of the 'petals'. Different typefaces are obtained by changing the daisywheel. This system gives low speed, high quality printing. *Dot matrix:* characters are created as a pattern of dots by a matrix of pins and transferred to paper. The quality of print depends on the number of pins in the print head and how often it can pass over the same line (slightly offset). Some dot-matrix printers can produce 'near letter quality' (NLQ) print but in general this system gives high-speed, low quality, printing. *Laser:* increasingly popular as their prices have reduced, these quiet printers produce the best quality hard copies at top speed.

*Software.* The term for programs which give instructions to the *Central processing unit.*

*Visual display unit.* A piece of hardware like a TV screen which displays input to and output from the computer.

## IT applications

The all-pervasive micro-chip has already influenced the areas of text and data processing, and communications. I will describe several of its main applications and then give an assessment of usage. Owing to a lack of precise statistics in this field, it is difficult to build up a really accurate picture. There are, however, some interesting trends.

## Word processors

The principal function of a word processor is to receive, process, store and retrieve large quantities of text at high speed. Word processing systems fall into three main categories:

- *Stand alone* or *dedicated.* Each machine is a self-contained unit with its own printer, floppy disks, VDU, internal processing unit and software. These machines are ideal for the production of large reports and standardised letters. Through storage on floppy disks, they have almost infinite memories and are therefore best suited to the bulk production of text.
- *Shared resource.* Each VDU is linked to a central processing unit. This system (sometimes called a Local Area Network) is less expensive than a stand alone because one processor is shared by several users. However, some experts feel it is less effective, particularly for bulk work, because the central processor slows down or even jams when heavy demands are placed on it at the same time. It is therefore a system best suited to intermittent use.
- *Personal computer.* By insertion of a special program or software these machines can be used for word processing. Now that personal computers have larger memories they are more useful for word processing, but may not be as effective as the stand alone for bulk production. The big advantage of this flexible self-contained system is that it can be used for text and data processing, as well as communications. By changing the software, you have available a whole range of different applications. Many secretaries using personal computers become information gatherers and can be involved in tasks outside their former province. This can be attractive to those secretaries wishing to expand their role. The continuing increase in word processing software sales indicates that PCs and laptop computers are being used more for this task.

## Electronic typewriters

These have all but replaced the market for electric (and manual) typewriters, although many firms keep their old electric and manual machines as stand-bys.

Why have electronic typewriters been so successful?

- They cost less than electric typewriters because they are quicker and cheaper to make. Their smaller power pack and design lend themselves to automated assembly with the result that factories can

137

produce three electronic typewriters in the time it would take to produce a single electric one.

- They are more reliable than electric typewriters because they have fewer moving parts to go wrong.
- They are very flexible and some can be turned into fully-fledged word processors. The typewriter is linked, via a computer interface, to a micro-computer, screen, software and floppy disks. In this new arrangement, the typewriter becomes the printer, while the micro-computer is used as the main text keyboard. The beauty of this system is its complete adaptability in that extra facilities can be added, funds and demand permitting.

Virtually all electronic typewriters now have built-in memory and editing facilities similar to those of a simple word processor. Most display the current typing line (at least) allowing corrections to be made before they appear on the paper and some even check your spelling. An immaculate carbon is only one bonus of these machines.

## Electronic mail

Electronic mail is the overall term given to describe the transmission of text electronically. Despatched information can be shown in one of two ways:

- Automatically on a computer or word processing terminal, with no paper copies involved; or
- Conventionally on a paper copy by means of teletex, facsimile, word processor or electronic typewriter. Suitably converted telex machines can also be used.

Both methods represent electronic mail – the difference between them is whether a paper copy is produced as a result of transmission.

Generally speaking, the first method is used for sending urgent and brief messages between inter-company executives who have their own computer terminals. This is a cheap and efficient form of communication which reduces reliance on the telephone. Depending on the sophistication of the transmission equipment, there may be an electronic 'mailbox' where messages can be stored until their recipient indicates that he or she is ready to receive them. This method is particularly helpful for those executives who:

- Do not have a secretary;
- Spend time away from their desks;
- Are a one-man business who can link in to an electronic mailbox by means of a PC or laptop computer and any telephone, whenever they are away from base;

- Where time zones are involved.

The second method is normally used for sending lengthy and/or external communications where paper copies are necessary, eg letters, reports etc.

E-mail has flourished with the boom in the use of micro-computers. At present E-mail systems have about 100,000 users in the UK. Several services are currently licensed to operate in the UK, the main three being Telecom Gold, One-to-One and Mercury Link 7500. The main advantages of E-mail are:

- Speed. 1500 characters can be transmitted in less than 10 seconds;
- You can use all the characters on a normal keyboard;
- Your boss can send/receive messages wherever he happens to be on the telephone network, provided he has a laptop computer and acoustic coupler or plug-in telephone connection. Any messages can be left in a 'mailbox' which only the other party can access, so you don't *both* need to be available at the same time in order to pass messages.

One disadvantage which E-mail services share with telex is that they cannot be used for sending or receiving pictures or diagrams. However, the most awkward problem lies in the lack of satisfactory compatibility between the different services which prevents subscribers of one system readily communicating with subscribers of another. However, there are currently moves afoot to resolve this so that private office E-mail, fax, telex and mailbox services can be interconnected.

## Telex

Telex remains popular with over 100,000 users in the UK and about 2 million worldwide.

Modern telex machines are no longer the loud chattering devices of yesteryear which had to be placed in a separate room so as not to distract employees from other tasks. Today's telex machines resemble office computers and usually have their own word processing facilities so that messages can be easily composed and edited on a VDU before transmission. They may also have memory banks which allow a directory of most frequently used telex numbers to be stored. The machine is then programmed to dial the required number automatically at a press of the company name. Some machines will redial an engaged telex number or will alert you if they have been unable to transmit.

Alternatively, a 'telex box' can be connected to your office computer enabling this to be used as a telex machine. A separate telex line will be required for linking to the networks operated by BT or Mercury.

Electronic mail users can also send telexes via their interfaces to the telex networks.

The limitations of telex, when compared to facsimile and E-mail, lie in its restricted vocabulary (only capital letters and reduced punctuation) and speed (it takes nearly four minutes to transmit 1500 characters). It cannot be used for sending plans or diagrams, and the longer the message the more expensive it becomes.

## Teletex

Teletex was launched by BT a few years ago and is not to be confused with Teletext which allows pages of text material to be displayed on suitably equipped television sets, eg CEEFAX, ORACLE (broadcast teletext) or PRESTEL (interactive teletext).

Teletex allows the fast transmission of text and data via either:

the Public Switched Telephone Network (PSTN): the normal telephone networks operated by BT and Mercury; or

the Public Data Network (PDN): a network for transmitting data at higher speeds than can be achieved over PSTN. BT's PDN is known as the Packet Switchstream Network.

The drawback with teletex is that there are only a few hundred users in the UK and no interconnection facilities between the PSTN and the PDN for teletex users. Customers are only able to send messages to other teletex users on the same network. Although teletex is operational in more than 20 countries the service has yet to take off in the UK.

## Facsimile

The facsimile, or fax, resembles a photocopier but with the addition of an attached telephone. Any document can be fed straight into the machine and an exact replica will be transmitted to a recipient fax machine. It therefore eliminates the need for:

- A specialist operator (it is as straightforward to use as a photocopier);
- The hand delivery of documents when presentation is important, eg signatures on contracts.

Many of the world's great institutions have taken advantage of this speedy despatch of accurate text, data and pictures, especially the police, the press and military establishments and virtually all medium/large companies now have a facsimile facility. People even order take-away meals and request records on the radio by fax these days! Fax overtook telex as the most popular data transmission service in 1986 and is still growing fast with around 400,000 users in the UK and more than 3.5 million worldwide at the beginning of the 1990s.

Copies are normally produced on special thermal paper but some modern machines use plain paper. This is better as thermal paper is expensive and the print fades with time.

Over the years, in order to increase the speed of fax transmissions, three different standard speeds have evolved through international agreement.

*Group 1* - transmits/receives an A4 page in about 6 minutes (now virtually obsolete);
*Group 2* - transmits/receives an A4 page in about 3 minutes;
*Group 3* - transmits/receives an A4 page in under 1 minute.

In practice most machines now available for purchase or lease are Group 3 types. Group 3 machines can normally communicate with other machines by transmitting at slower speeds. Group 4 machines, capable of transmitting an A4 sheet in 3 seconds, have recently come into operation but these only work over the PDN and not via normal telephone lines. For the more common Group 3 machines transmission quality over the PSTN is likely to improve consistently as all the public networks become digital.

### Telex and facsimile bureaux
If your company cannot justify the expense of its own telex/fax equipment for occasional messages, you can use the services of the many bureaux available. Consult the Yellow Pages or Business Pages (under Fax/Telex Bureaux) for details of your nearest firm.

### Local area networks (LANs) or multi-user systems
Local area networks enable several micro-computers and/or word processors to be linked to a single computer. Each desktop terminal may have some processing capability itself or may simply be the means for linking several users into the central processor. If all company employees are linked in this way, the paperless office can become a reality. The use of a LAN means that:

- Several people in different locations (even different cities) can have access to centrally stored data;
- Staff can generate their own text and data, and can communicate, one terminal to another;
- Use of resources can be streamlined and communications between people improved;
- Giving employees access to common information via their terminal

141

can make the production of internal memos and reports a thing of the past.

It is said (by manufacturers, no doubt!) that managers in such an environment spend very little time on support functions and devote themselves almost entirely to their proper job – that of managing. By the same token, secretaries with their own terminals can eliminate much of their routine to become real PAs.

Offices with LANs are still comparatively rare in the UK but there will be more as time goes on. However, we have a long way to go before this sophisticated equipment becomes commonplace.

## Optical disks

Optical disks are now available which provide an alternative method of storage to the floppy disks still widely used at present. Some experts are worried that floppy disks, which work on a magnetic principle, are not totally reliable for storing information. Optical disks are more effective in that data are stored and retrieved by means of a low-level laser beam. The average optical disk, which looks like a CD, can store 500,000 pages of information and is unaffected by dust or fingerprints. However, at present, writing data on to disks and reading from them is slower than using magnetic media systems and the majority are the 'Write Once Read Many' (WORM) variety which means that they cannot be erased and used again. They are, though, suitable for archiving purposes – the end of that filing cabinet may be in sight.

## Laser printers

The laser printer is an innovation which makes paper copies direct from stored data. The copies are excellent and almost of letterpress quality. With advances in computer software which enable graphs and charts to be produced with a keyboard and screen, it becomes simplicity itself using a laser printer to make presentation quality copies. This avoids the need to use specialist artists when producing top quality reports and slides.

The cost of laser printers is still fairly high but competition in this market is rife and consequently prices are falling. As a result more and more companies are using these machines to prepare their own 'in-house' reports, documents and correspondence (80,000 were sold in the UK in 1989 alone).

## Is IT a job threat?

Despite the very rapid take-up of IT over the past decade by businesses large and small there is no firm evidence that its introduction is a job threat. In fact, the most recent (1990) statistics show that the proportion of administrative, technical and clerical workers (including secretaries) has remained roughly the same (and in some industries actually increased) in recent years. And the results of a government survey conducted in 1989/90 ('Skills Needs in Britain') found that secretaries and clerical workers were among the occupations causing the most recruitment difficulties.

Social and demographic changes are likely to have a more significant effect on secretarial jobs than IT in the next decade. Between 1990 and the turn of the century the number of men in the labour force is projected to remain static (15.9 million) but the number of women is projected to increase by 700,000 to 12.9 million when women are expected to constitute 45.6 per cent of the workforce. A large proportion of these are expected to be those women who are combining a family with a career. In 1984 27 per cent of women with children under five continued to work; by 1989 this was 40 per cent and the figure is still rising. Since nearly one-third of working women are employed in secretarial/office jobs it seems likely that there will be increased competition for these jobs in the next decade. On the other hand, the number of young people (16–24) entering the job market will continue to fall by a further 1.1 million by the year 2001. So graduate secretaries and college leavers are likely to be in great demand!

The employers and secretarial agencies I have spoken to have agreed that there were fewer secretarial jobs around in the early 1990s, probably because of the recession. Companies cut back to their minimal requirements, awaiting more prosperous times. The consensus is that companies are beginning to hire more secretaries, but it also appears that competition for secretarial jobs is greater now than ever before.

What about the impact of IT? It has been said that technology is labour saving but does not eliminate work – there are too many tasks to which its versatility can be applied. To assume therefore that job losses are the inevitable result of IT is an oversimplification of a complex issue.

## Is IT a role threat?

The use of a new office technology can affect the role of the secretary in three different ways:

### 1. More of a PA

If IT is used as a complementary tool, it can free secretaries from time-consuming drudgery so that they can become true PAs. They will have more time for administration and support functions to ensure that the office runs like clockwork and their boss can make best use of his working

143

day. This is, after all, what secretarial work is all about.

IT can also enable secretaries to become more involved in the organisation of their company. By using data programs on a PC, the secretary can assimilate and present the information her boss needs for briefings and meetings. Taking this one step further, she can produce company information for a number of people by writing reports and making recommendations. She can thereby become an executive in her own right. This type of role has become commonplace in the United States where secretaries undertake more of their bosses' routine tasks. Freeing management in this way is rewarding for secretaries, and makes good business sense.

In another area of administration, secretaries are ideally placed to handle the installation of IT. They have the experience to know what is needed and why, and can apply this to feasibility studies and recommendations for management. Many secretaries have undertaken such tasks and found that they have become responsible for the budgeting and organisational aspects of IT once installed. This can lead to an executive job of its own.

Not all secretaries wish to develop their roles in the ways described but it is all to the good that opportunities are there for those with the right motivation.

## 2. Keyboard queen

IT could adversely affect the role of the secretary by tying her to a keyboard more than before so as to maximise the use of expensive equipment. The text editing facility can sometimes encourage managers to request endless drafts of the same report. This is frustrating for the secretary who spends more time at the keyboard for an identical end product; and it is an expensive waste of time for her manager. Unfortunately, many managers do not fully understand IT and focus too much on its text editing facilities. Secretaries thus afflicted need to educate their bosses about the machines' versatility (and their own).

By the same token, the use of IT can make some executives think that the impossible is always at the end of a button. Secretaries can find themselves working long hours on emergency reports which would not have been attempted with conventional equipment. IT is no more a magical solution to unrealistic deadlines than an ordinary typewriter was when first invented.

## 3. Shared secretary

An increasing trend has been the use of the shared secretary. Even at the most senior level, many PAs now work for several executives where in the past they would have worked for only one. This is a disappointing 'development'. One of the most attractive features of word processing is freedom from repetitive typing. If, however, the time saved is merely deployed to handle the typing of more people, you would be better off with a typewriter.

Why has this trend arisen? The cost-conscious employer, perhaps having incurred the heavy expenditure of IT, may well view the shared secretary as the most financially effective method of staff deployment. On paper he seems to be saving money. However, it is in the area of management that the real cost savings are to be made. A manager's time is far more expensive than that of a secretary. When IT enables a secretary to become a true PA, the company will benefit financially through the greater effectiveness of her boss. Freed from routine and administration, he has more time for his proper job – that of getting new cash business. The shared secretary is therefore a false economy.

Some people think that IT will put an end to the traditional secretarial skills of shorthand, layout and record-keeping (among 101 other things). It is undoubtedly true that the wider use of the dictaphone in recent years has brought about a decline in the use of shorthand. However, many employers still seek shorthand skills as they are considered to represent the traditional values of a first-class secretary. I think employers will become more demanding in the future and require a mixture of old and new skills.

Secretaries definitely need to be familiar with IT and would be well advised to get some broad-based training in business and information systems. The more strings you have to your bow, the better. IT offers a challenge, and an improvement to the working environment, but only if you are prepared to understand and use it. Some employers have found that the most competent secretaries were reluctant to learn about IT because they felt they already did an excellent job. While this is probably true, none of us can afford to ignore IT.

The sophisticated kinds of IT, primarily Local Area Networks, can, by their very nature, completely change the role of the secretary. In these cases, each secretary has a work-station which links her with all or part of the computerised office systems. There are facilities for electronic diaries, booking meetings, electronic mail, and text and data processing.

The most important thing about IT is that secretaries should, wherever possible, take the initiative in developing their own role. If they fail to do this, they could find their jobs being shaped by the equipment.

## Is IT an intellectual threat?

No machine yet invented has the intellectual abilities of the human brain. Even the most sophisticated processors are incapable of performing their tasks unless someone gives them the commands. In no way, therefore, is IT an intellectual threat.

As for learning the skills to use IT, the basic criteria for most of these are an ability to type and user interest. The latter point is very important. It has been found that the take-up rate for learning IT is more related to interest than anything else. Suspicion and hostility are the most effective barriers to learning. Some older secretaries may be a little more hesitant about using the equipment at first, but given that the interest is there, they should have no problems in coping. Indeed, mature secretaries with conventional and IT skills, and sound working experience, are likely to be much in demand. They have the most to offer an employer.

IT can be a daunting prospect for secretaries returning to work after a long break. Many organisations and local authorities do offer training courses which can help to put returners on the right track – details are given on page 157.

## Is IT a health threat?

There is a wealth of material around suggesting that there may be a link between the use of IT and certain health problems. The following information has been extracted (predominantly) from an excellent guide to the subject produced by City Centre entitled *VDU Hazards Factpack*. The factpack is updated regularly and can be obtained from: City Centre, 32–35 Featherstone Street, London EC1Y 8QX; tel 071-608 1338 (price £3).

### Eyes and vision

The most commonly reported ill effects of VDU work are those associated with the eyes and vision. Eighty per cent of VDU workers report problems mainly involved their eyesight. These problems include eyestrain, sore eyes/irritated eyes, blurred vision, changes in colour perception, tiredness/irritability, headaches, migraine, nausea and discomfort with contact lenses.

What are the causes? Low humidity may cause discomfort to contact lens wearers. Screen glare and reflection are a known cause of eyestrain and headaches. Not only is it in an employer's interest to provide a glare-free environment – staff will work more effectively and with fewer problems – it may also become a legal responsibility on 1 January 1993, when an EC directive on health and safety requirements at work comes into effect. The directive specifies that all screens shuld have brightness and contrast controls, as well as a tilt and swivel mechanism. Flickering screens, often caused by low refresh rates, can trigger migraines as well as causing irritation and stress. In order to comply with the EC directive all monitors must be free of flicker and the distortion that often occurs towards the corners of the screen. Furthermore, every VDU operator will have the right to eye tests before starting screen work and at any time he or she experiences eyesight problems.

Further information and advice can be obtained from the Association of Optometrists who produce a free booklet entitled *Your Eyes and VDUs*, which covers lighting, positioning of equipment, screens and filters as well as general information on the relationship between eyesight and VDU work. Contact: The Eye Care Information Bureau, 4 Ching Court, Shelton Street, London WC2H 9DG. 'Better Lighting at Work' is a pamphlet which gives an overview of lighting requirements for VDU work and a list of companies offering expert advice on the subject. It can be obtained free from the Lighting Industry Federation, 207 Balham High Road, London SW17 7BQ; tel 081-675 5432.

## Repetitive Strain Injury (RSI)

RSI is a multi-symptom disorder which can include one or any combination of the following: carpel tunnel syndrome, tendonitis and tenosynovitis. All affect the wrist of long-term VDU keyboard operators causing a breakdown in the natural lubrication of the tendons which leads to inflammation, numbing, cramps and even audible creaking. Other related symptoms include backache and neck ache, lack of movement in the arms, shooting pains and, at an advanced state, partial paralysis.

Historically, RSI has been the curse of those employed on the shop floor in heavy industry – production line and machine operators. Musicians, cleaners and hairdressers are also sufferers. More recently white collar VDU/keyboard operators have been affected. When it started to cripple the careers of prominent journalists, the issue found a national voice. The *Financial Times* has been hit hardest, over 100 journalists being referred to the company's doctor with symptoms.

There are now initiatives to implement legal guidelines in an attempt to prevent an increase in RSI sufferers. In Australia, unions have negotiated an agreement with employers to restrict the number of keystrokes to under 10,000 an hour – how this is to be effectively implemented remains to be seen. Proper office equipment and correct keyboard posture can help. A company called Maltron claims to have designed a keyboard which actually combats RSI.

Further information can be obtained from:

- The Employment Committee of the City Women's Network who have compiled a six-page pamphlet covering many aspects of the ailment. The paper also contains notes on who is entitled to sue whom under common law for injury sustained on the job and an employer's statutory obligations are also listed. Contact: City Women's Network; tel 081-569 2351.

- City Centre produces a booklet entitled *An Office Worker's Guide to Repetitive Strain Injury* which provides guidance and advice on getting medical help, rights at work, pursuing compensation claims and preventing RSI, in addition to describing the range of RSI's causes and symptoms. The booklet, which costs £3, is available from City Centre, 32–35 Featherstone Street, London EC1Y 8QX; tel 071-608 1338.

- The Health and Safety Executive has recently published a guide to RSI for employers entitled *Work Related Upper Limb Disorders – A Guide to Prevention*, available price £3.45 from HMSO.

- A support group for sufferers (and for general advice on information) is run by Wendy Lawrence, Nottingham RSI Support Group, 26 Balmoral Road, Colwick, Nottinghamshire.

## Skin complaints

For a number of years many VDU workers have been reporting to their doctors, health and safety representatives, employers etc with skin complaints from which they had not suffered prior to working with VDUs. Complaints include acne, rosacea, seborrhoeic and atopic dermatitis, talangiectases, pustulosis, urticaria, otitis and various mild irritations.

Some surveys indicate that many of these conditions develop a few months after starting VDU work. Other surveys have found clusters of skin complaints among office workers who do not work with, or near, VDUs. This suggests that the office environment itself may be the problem.

There has been much speculation as to the causes of this apparent link between VDU work and skin complaints. The most likely explanation seems to be a combination of inadequate ventilation, an over-dry atmosphere and excessive static electricity. Most air-conditioning systems were not designed to cope with the extra heat generated by VDUs which results in low humidity levels. Usually a complete overhaul of the air-conditioning and ventilation system is needed to rectify the problem. To reduce static electricity nylon carpets should be avoided or regularly treated with an anti-static fluid. Static from the VDU screen itself may be temporarily controlled by the use of anti-static solution or wipes. Anti-static filters can be fitted to VDU screens as a long-term solution.

The nature of the relationship between VDU work and skin rashes is still not known, so it is not clear whether these steps will eliminate or reduce the incidence of skin problems among VDU workers. Further information can be obtained from a leaflet on skin rashes which is part of the *VDU Hazards Factpack* published by City Centre (see page 146 for address).

## Pregnancy

Most women who work with VDUs are now aware that a link has been established between VDU usage and miscarriage/birth abnormality. However tenuous this may be, it is clear that there is cause for concern.

The issue first came to the attention of the media in 1979 when four out of seven pregnancies within the space of one year in the classified department of the *Toronto Star* newspaper in Canada resulted in babies being born with deformities. These women all used VDUs extensively in their work. Since then there have been many clusters of miscarriages and birth defects reported by women from all over the world who use VDUs.

The evidence is inconclusive. For example, the California Kaiser Permanente Medical Care Program in Oakland conducted a survey in 1988 which established an increase in miscarriages during the first three months of pregnancy among women working more than half the working week on a VDU. Two years earlier the Swedish Trade Union Confederation found an increased level of congenital malformations (especially of the heart) among offspring of VDU workers. There have been many other similar surveys – some concluding that VDU work was to blame, others deciding it wasn't. The University of Manchester Institute of Science and Technology, for example, in a study carried out in 1991 on 3500 workers at the Inland Revenue, concluded that pregnant women working with VDUs did not suffer a higher miscarriage rate than non-VDU workers. They *did*, however, note a correlation between VDU work and high stress levels.

What are the possible causes?

- *Posture.*1 It is well established that bad posture can contribute towards early miscarriage. Since many VDU workers have to sit in front of the screen for four or more hours a day this could contribute to the high incidence of miscarriage that some studies have revealed. However, this does not explain why typists sitting for many hours at electric typewriters do not suffer a higher incidence of miscarriage. Nor does this hypothesis address the issue of birth abnormality.
- *Stress.* It is generally accepted that intense stress can precipitate a miscarriage and that lower levels of stress over a period of time can induce abnormal hormonal activity and high blood pressure which

can result in complications during pregnancy. It is with these facts in mind that researchers have studied the whole working environment and job content of VDU users to determine whether or not they experience higher stress levels than, say, typists and clerical workers in non-automated jobs.

Factors which tend to cause stress to VDU workers include bad overhead lighting (often too bright causing glare), inappropriate air-conditioning and heating systems for VDU work, and unsuitable chairs and tables. Other factors include insufficient training, prolonged machine response time, close supervision, heavy workload, electronic monitoring, under-use of skills, repetitive and boring tasks, and the absence of management understanding of, and sympathy with, these problems. These factors can combine to put VDU operators under extreme stress.

Research has shown that people using VDUs in a professional capacity (eg programmers, analysts, writers) do not suffer from new technology-related stress to the same extent as, for example, data processors. This suggests that VDU-induced stress probably owes less to ergonomic factors (lighting, seating etc) than to human factors (repetitive, boring tasks, under-use of skills). To this extent a true 'secretary' (rather than simply a glorified typist) should not suffer extra stress owing to the introduction of IT.

It is difficult to quantify stress objectively since much depends on the individual's response. What one person finds stressful, another will not. It therefore seems unlikely that stress alone could account for the high miscarriage rate among VDU users, although it could well be a contributory factor.

- *Radiation.* There are two types of radiation – ionising and non-ionising. Both are emitted at detectable levels from most VDUs. The table opposite shows the types of radiation, how they are used and the main sources of such radiation. The most common type of VDU is the cathode-ray tube which produces ionising radiation; its various electronic components produce non-ionising radiation.

It is known that ionising radiation changes the structure of cells, produces cancer, sterility, cataracts, birth defects and miscarriage. This can happen even when exposure is at a very low level.

Studies in the USA have revealed that some VDUs, particularly older models, leak ionising radiation. The current controversy is over what level of radiation is harmful to our bodies. The standards for exposure set in most western countries are based on the most common form of cathode-ray tube technology – the TV set. However, most people do not sit 18 inches away from their TV for seven to eight hours a day.

| Extra low frequency | Radio frequencies | Microwaves | Infrared | VISIBLE LIGHT | Ultraviolet | Soft x-ray | Hard x-ray gamma rays |
|---|---|---|---|---|---|---|---|
| High voltage lines VDU | Radio, CB TV VDU | Radar Microwave ovens VDU | Sun VDU | | Sun VDU | Medical x-ray TV VDU | Nuclear fall-out |
| Non-ionising radiation | | | | | Ionising radiation | | |

Little information is available on the biological effects of non-ionising radiation. Recent research has produced evidence which clearly links exposure to extra low frequency waves to biological damage in animals. Both Roger Coghill in his book *Electro-pollution* and Paul Brodeur in *Currents of Death: Power Lines, Computer Terminals and the Attempt to Cover Up Their Threat to Your Health* assert that there is a threat to humans from extra low frequency waves.

Given that the threat is possible, but not yet proved, different countries have reacted in different ways. In Scandinavia and West Germany pressure from labour movements has meant that employers are effectively obliged to use low radiation equipment. Sweden, in particular, has adopted a particular set of standards laid down by the National Institute of Radiation Protection (SSI). Many major manufacturers such as Philips, IBM, Taxan and Hitachi are now offering SSI standard monitors to the UK and US markets. Also appearing on the market are liquid crystal display (LCD) monitors which do not give off the radiation associated with cathode-ray tubes. Scandinavian manufacturers are quietly confident that the SSI standard will come to be accepted by the EC, in which case most monitors in current use would be banned.

A compromise solution is to add safety devices to existing equipment and, while enterprising suppliers are offering everything from eye goggles to lead aprons, the most popular choice is a protective screen. This device, although gaining popularity in the UK (and virtually a legal requirement in the USA where fear of litigation has prompted action from employers), is a rather dubious solution since most radiation comes from the sides and back of the VDU. In fact, the World Health Organisation has recommended that no one should sit within one metre of the back or sides of a

VDU. The simplest solution is to arrange the office so no one has to sit directly behind a VDU, and perhaps add a filter to the screen.

Meanwhile, if you are planning to have a baby and you are concerned about the possible effects of working with IT you could:

- Ask to be transferred to alternative work or to return to using 'old' electric/electronic typewriters temporarily;
- Avoid unnecessary exposure to VDUs – take coffee and lunch breaks away from the machine;
- Report any unusual medical symptoms to your health and safety officer and/or doctor;
- Ask your employer for details of the equipment's specifications. Is the flyback transformer (the end of the cathode-ray tube which leaks most radiation) shielded?
- If you use an older model (pre-1977), try to find out whether it contains polychlorinated bi-phenyls (PCBs). These insulating fluids were sometimes used in 'old' VDUs. Since PCBs are known to be hazardous to health your employer has a duty under the Health and Safety at Work Act to obtain this information.
- Contact City Centre (address on page 146) for further advice or information.

### Stress

For many people stress at work is something normally associated with high-powered executives. Stress is now recognised as an occupational disease suffered by many workers, particularly those performing repetitive, boring jobs. Stress is rapidly becoming a major problem for VDU users.

Stress is commonly described as the 'fight or flight' syndrome and is used to describe the changes which occur in the body as the nervous system prepares for action, with a discharge of adrenalin and an increase in heart rate, blood pressure and digestive juices. If not dissipated this stress leads to fatigue, irritability and depression, headaches, migraine, nausea, sleeplessness, menstrual problems and accidents in the short term. In the long term, stress can lead to heart disease, high blood pressure, stomach problems, depression, anxiety, dermatitis, ulcers and fertility problems.

Most of the causes of stress associated with VDU work were outlined in the section on pregnancy. There are no easy short-term solutions to the problems of stress. Good job design, regular breaks and a ban on monitoring will help to reduce stress levels if combined with the ergonomic measures outlined above. In addition, comfortable, pleasant rest rooms should be available for people to spend their breaks in.

City Centre produces a booklet entitled *Stress and VDU Work*, price £1.50, which deals in greater detail with the symptoms, effects, consequences and causes of stress and has a useful section on tackling workplace stress. Write or phone City Centre, see page 146.

## Ozone from laser printers and photocopiers

Ozone is a toxic substance which can cause throat irritation, coughing, headaches and chest pains. The sources of ozone in offices are photocopiers and laser printers. Ideally these should be housed in a separate well-ventilated room. However, as photocopiers have become smaller and quieter they are more likely to be dotted around offices among working people. The same is true of the fast, quiet laser printers. There is no incentive to site them in separate rooms.

In Denmark, where the noxious effect of ozone has been recognised for some time, more than 50 per cent of laser printers are fitted with an add-on ozone filter. Copiers and laser printers are all fitted with internal carbon filters which break down the ozone, but with age the filters become clogged with dust (more quickly if ventilation is poor) and become inefficient. Neither manufacturers nor suppliers mention this. The filters can (usually) be changed or, alternatively, add-on filters can now be purchased for around £300–£400. To enquire about an add-on filter contact: INCOTEL, PO Box 311, London N3; tel 081-343 1401.

## Workers' Rights Campaign

The VDU Workers' Rights Campaign was set up by City Centre in 1985 to campaign for changes in the law in the belief that legislation on VDU usage and safety would help trade unionists in their negotiations and would help to protect unionised VDU workers. The campaign has extensive parliamentary and trade union support. Its demands are:

- Limit work with a VDU to four hours within any working day or 50 per cent of the working time, whichever is shorter. And further, limit the maximum period of continuous work to one hour, to be followed by a 15-minute break away from the unit.
- Specify design requirements to VDU manufacturers, and VDU work station design and layout to minimise visual, postural and ergonomic stress.
- Require compulsory shielding of all VDUs to eliminate electro-magnetic radiation emissions.
- Establish the right of VDU workers to transfer to other work when planning to start or add to their family.

Some of these demands are already accepted in other countries where the health problems caused by VDU work are treated seriously by governments.

City Centre advises individuals on VDU hazards, gives talks to trade union branches and workplace groups, gives advice to unions and staff groups on VDU health and safety agreements, and loans videos on VDUs to groups. The Centre produces a quarterly health and safety bulletin which keeps readers up to date with the latest research and information – contact City Centre for subscription details (address on page 146).

## Further information on health aspects of VDU work

The Work Research Unit of the Advisory, Conciliation and Arbitration Service will provide a free bibliography of current IT health and safety research. The address is listed in the Appendix, or phone the information service on 071-210 3895. Following is a list of some recent publications on the subject.

*Ergonomics in Computerized Offices* by E Grandjean published by Taylor and Francis, London (1987).

'Health and safety at work' by Meaghan Botterill in *Management Services* (Vol 34, No 4, April 1990, pp 6–10). This article is concerned with the changes that will take place in 1992 with regard to the implications and implementation of European directives affecting British industry, particularly health and safety in the workplace.

'Health at work – are pregnant women different?' in *Labour Research* (Vol 79, No 3, March 1990, pp 15–16) discusses health and safety policies concerning pregnant women. The article argues that pregnant workers lose out by being removed from potential hazards, screening them out of particular jobs. It also means that the hazards tend not to be dealt with.

'Looking good' by Derek Glick in *Occupational Safety and Health* (Vol 19, No 4, April 1989, pp 16–18). The author – an optician – looks at just how important it is for operators of VDUs and machinery to have regular eye tests.

*Office Work and Your Health* by R Bramwell and M Davidson, published by the Inland Revenue Staff Federation, London (1990).

*The Office Workers' Guide to Sick Building Syndrome* (price £2.50) produced by City Centre, 32–35 Featherstone Street, London EC1X 8QX; tel 071-608 1338.

*Women's Health in the Office*, an information pack (price £2.50) produced by City Centre, 32–35 Featherstone Street, London EC1X 8QX; tel 071-608 1338.

*Working with Visual Display Units* published by the International Labour Office (1989) in the Occupational Safety and Health series (No 61).

'The VDU directive' by Richard Kidner in the *New Law Journal* (Vol 140, No 6485, 21 December 1990, pp 1795-6) looks at the future of office safety in the light of the EC directive.

*VDU Health and Safety.* Draft British Standard produced in 6 parts (1987):

| | | |
|---|---|---|
| 1 | General introduction | 87/40674 |
| 2 | Task requirement | 87/40675 |
| 3 | Visual display requirements | 87/40676 |
| 4 | Keyboard requirements | 87/40677 |
| 5 | Work station design | 87/40678 |
| 6 | Work environment | 87/40679 |

Available from: Sales Administration (Drafts), British Standards Institution, Linford Wood, Milton Keynes MK14 6LE, price £7.50 (£3 to BSI members) for each part.

'Visual display terminals: health issues and productivity' by E-B Chapnik and C Gross in *Personnel*, May 1987, pp 10-16.

## Is IT a financial threat?

It appears that the present demand for word processing secretaries outstrips supply, and salaries are therefore high. In many instances they have become sufficiently inflated to be on a par with, or even above, those of the top PAs.

If your company introduces IT it is unlikely that you will be paid a higher salary for working it. Employers who have borne the cost of sophisticated capital equipment and staff training appear reluctant to incur the additional cost of a salary review. However, you can console yourself with having learnt a completely new and marketable skill for free. This is an important consideration when viewed against the costs of private word processing/technology courses. When you make a change of job, you will undoubtedly be able to earn a better salary with this new skill.

A word of caution though – word processing salaries are likely to drop once there are a sufficient number of trained users on the job market. Given that up-and-coming generations are familiar with keyboards and computers almost from babyhood, the competition for IT jobs will increase as salaries fall.

## New technology case study: British Telecom

While pockets of the company are still organised on traditional lines, most of BT is progressing towards the paperless office. How have staff adjusted to the change?

155

BT's secretarial recruitment officer told me that there have not been any secretarial job losses as a direct result of new technology and staff have adapted well. College leavers and junior secretaries have been particularly enthusiastic – to such an extent that some have not used a typewriter since joining. A few of BT's senior secretaries showed some initial hesitancy in using the new equipment but the supervisor of typing put this down to an attitude of mind rather than a skills problem. Once trained, the senior secretaries were just as adept as the rest – and enthusiastic too.

All BT secretaries have access to word processors, and those staff based at their City of London headquarters are linked to all kinds of electronic wizardry via a Local Area Network. The technology has been a great success among secretaries who may now have more time to devote to the administrative side of their role.

In the use of new technology BT has adopted a caring approach within their safety guidelines. All full-time VDU operators may take a 15-minute break away from the machines after two hours' continuous use, and are offered eye tests at the Occupational Health Clinic every six months. Occasional VDU operators and secretaries may have eye tests as and when they like.

Word processors are sited in accordance with individual preferences and each machine has its own adjustable brightness control. While there is no conclusive evidence at this time to link a health risk with the use of VDUs during pregnancy, BT are sufficiently flexible to try to accommodate a move to a different area if this is necessary for the emotional well-being of the individual concerned.

## Sources of information

Some periodicals covering information technology:

- *What's New in Computing* (the monthly guide to products in data processing) – annual UK subscription £50, but some free subscriptions are available to executives working in the industry. Details from: *What's New in Computing*, Morgan Grampian Ltd, 30 Calderwood Street, London SE18 6QH; tel 071-855 7777.
- *Office Equipment News* – annual subscription £20, but some free subscriptions available to executives and administrators who buy or specify office equipment or services. Details from: *Office Equipment News*, MBC Publications Ltd, Audit House, Field End Road, Eastcote, Ruislip, Middlesex HA4 9LT; tel 081-868 4499.
- *Office Equipment Index* – annual subscription £45.00 but free copies available to qualifying executives responsible for buying office

equipment and materials. Details from: *Office Equipment Index*, EMAP, Maclaren House, 19 Scarbrook Road, Croydon, Surrey CR9 1QH; tel 081-688 7788; telex 946665; fax 081-688 8375/9300.

- *Business Equipment Digest* (incorporating *Business Systems and Equipment*) – annual subscription £30 (11 issues) but some free issues available. Details from: IML Techpress, Northside House, 69 Tweedy Road, Bromley, Kent BR1 3UT; tel 081-290 6666.

Most of these publications offer a free reader enquiry service under which they will arrange for you to receive information on products, services etc described in the journal. More publications are listed under Acknowledgements (page 158).

## Information technology associations

- The Office Automation Specialist Group of the British Computer Society is a network of professionals with an interest in office automation. The group distributes regular newsletters; holds meetings; organises specialist working groups and prepares briefing sheets on special subjects. Details of membership from: Graham Haffenden, Events Secretary, Office Automation Specialist Group, British Computer Society, 13 Mansfield Street, London W1M 0BP; 071-637 0471. Also at 14 Tara Court, 6 Court Downs Road, Beckenham, Kent BR3 2TG (home); tel 071-260 4448 (work).
- Women's Computer Centre Ltd is a voluntary organisation which offers information, courses, advice and a drop-in facility for women interested in learning more about computers. Details from: Rose Maxwell (Co-ordinator), Wesley House, 3rd Floor, 4 Wild Court, Holborn, London WC2B 5AU; tel 071-430 0112.

## Technology training

If you want to find out about technology training (word processing, micro-computing etc), there are three main sources of information (assuming you are self-funded):

- *Private secretarial colleges.* Your local newspaper or Yellow Pages will probably give the information you need. Costs for such courses are pretty steep, being the market rate. Obviously costs vary in accordance with the course content and length.
- *Local education authorities.* Many now run part-time day and/or evening courses which are (usually) heavily subsidised. Your local Adult Education Department will advise you.
- *Secretarial employment agencies.* Many now run word processing and/ or computing courses. Some of these agencies are: Alfred Marks

Bureau, Brook Street Bureau, Kelly Girl Services and Just Your Type.

Terms vary, so consult your nearest branch for details.

## Acknowledgements (information technology)

Central Statistics Office (1990) *Annual Abstract of Statistics*, HMSO

City Centre 'Ozone – putting your health at risk', *Safer Office Bulletin* (February 1991)

City Centre *VDU Hazards Factpack*

Grundy, J and Rosenthal, S *Your Eyes and VDUs*

Jarrett, D (1984) *The Electronic Office: A Management Guide to the Office of the Future* (2nd edition) Gower Press

Shipside, S (December 1990) 'Deadly terminals', *Micro Decision*

Shipside, S (January 1991) 'Trouble at mill: repetitive stress injury is now poised to assault British industry', *Micro Decision*

# Chapter 10

# A Question of Attitude

## Giving your best

In the previous chapters we have discussed the practicalities of coping with a secretarial job. Almost more important than these, however, is the attitude of the person carrying them out. Some people have excellent skills but with the wrong state of mind they'll never be anything more than 'just another secretary'.

What are the contributory factors to the 'right' state of mind?

- Take a pride in your work (even if it's making the tea). Check everything you do and if it's not to your usual high standard, do it again.
- Be flexible in what you do. Unless it goes completely against the grain, be prepared to try your hand at anything which crops up in your job (within reason, of course). If you confine yourself within rigid demarcation lines, you'll never develop or learn anything new.

  Also, be flexible with your colleagues and offer a helping hand when they're under pressure. Never be too proud to muck in with the rest.
- Be adaptable in how you approach your work, and change your methods to suit the circumstances prevailing at the time.
- Be innovative. Just because office routine has plodded along in the same way for the past ten years, it doesn't necessarily mean it's right. Get the grey matter going and put forward new ideas (tactfully).
- Absorb information like a sponge (without becoming nosy). Be aware of what's going on around you and you'll be able to fit together the various pieces of the work jigsaw.
- Be alert and work with a lively mind. Take an interest in your work (however mundane it is).
- Be sufficiently motivated to banish boredom. During slack periods or when your boss is away, use the opportunity to catch up on routine and develop new systems. If you've exhausted these possibilities, offer to help someone else. But don't ever sit around

waiting for work – you'll end up being idle and resentful of working when you have to.

- Be multi-functional and learn to juggle several tasks at once.
- Be quizzical about why tasks need to be done, and how they interrelate with others.
- Communicate well with your boss and colleagues. Don't hoard information (unless it's confidential of course).
- Be determined and assertive without becoming aggressive.
- Have genuine confidence in your own abilities without becoming conceited.
- Be kind to yourself when you make mistakes – they're part of living. Rectify the situation and make amends, but don't tear yourself to shreds because you did something wrong. We all have our 'off' days.
- Don't rest on your laurels. Work should be a constant challenge with new things to learn all the time. If opportunities don't present themselves, go and seek them yourself!

In summary (after this long list of dos and don'ts) I'd say that the most important thing I've learnt in my secretarial career is that every job is really what you make it. Most successful (and happy) secretaries will tell you that the job they do now bears little relation to the one they started with. We all have the opportunity to put our own stamp on each job, and develop ourselves at the same time. Be enthusiastic and positive about the profession you've chosen and you'll never look back!

## Striking a balance

Strive for excellence in your career without becoming a workaholic. To help do this, try to keep your life in balance by ensuring that you have proper rest, relaxation and holidays. We all need a break! In a demanding job, you'll need to keep your private life running as smoothly as possible. While being the last to claim expertise on this subject, I'd like to give a few tips which might help:

- *Look after yourself.* Eat proper meals (not junk) and don't have too many late nights during the week.
- *Strike a balance with your partner.* Take turns with the household chores, or get a cleaning lady (funds permitting). Leave posh cooking and dinner parties until the weekend.
- *Get organised:*
  — Make lists in a small pocket notebook kept in your handbag;
  — Plan your evening meal menus on a weekly basis (you can do

this on the train if a commuter) so you're not always worried about supper.

— Have simple nutritious meals (not 'convenience') and forget about puddings. Fruit and cheese are better for you and easy to cook!

— Bulk buy once a month if possible (storage and freezer permitting).

— Have a day off occasionally to do batch cooking for the freezer (if you have one).

— Cut down on the ironing. Buy clothes which press easily (most linens and silks are murder!). Fold household linen as soon as it's dry.

— Keep all household bills in a (large) bulldog clip and write down due dates on your kitchen calendar.

— Sanctify your Saturday morning lie-in by asking the milkman if you can pay him monthly by cheque.

## Making the most of your career

While I don't recommend the formulation of a 'ten-year plan', it's nevertheless a very good idea to have some kind of career goal – we all need something to aim for! Make gradual steps up the career ladder, building solid experience as you go. Plan your job changes carefully and in accordance with your overall ambitions. Try not to blow with the wind.

Perhaps you aspire to management and wish to make a transitional move? In my view, there is no better basis to such a role than secretarial experience which will have taught you about:

● Office practice, management techniques and the business world (from a realistic standpoint);
● Common sense and logical application (we hope).

Try not to leave it too long before making the change – transferring from an essentially supportive role can be more difficult the longer it's left. Be prepared to start at the bottom of the career ladder again, and demonstrate your commitment by undertaking some part-time studies (such as the Diploma of Management Studies). This may necessitate an initial salary drop and some very hard spare-time work, but should be well worth it in the long run. (No one can expect a promising career on a plate.) These days you have to prove your worth to a potential employer, often against stiff graduate competition. However, you should take this in your stride if you are sufficiently ambitious.

If you remain a secretary, you might think about taking one of the many different secretarial diplomas at some stage (assuming you don't already have them all). Studying is always worthwhile but don't expect instant promotion because of it. Many employers feel that basic secretarial qualifications coupled with solid experience are what count most. So consider carefully.

However, I advise every secretary to keep up to date with new technology and learn as many operational skills as possible. Even the most senior PAs need to have a sound working knowledge of all the latest developments – they never know when they might need to brief their boss.

I wish you all the very best in your chosen career. There are great challenges ahead for secretaries today – we have only to rise to them!

# Appendix

## Equal Opportunities Commission

The Equal Opportunities Commission was established by Parliament in 1975 as an independent body whose function was, and is, to fight sex discrimination in all walks of life.

It offers an advisory service to individuals who may be uncertain of their rights under the Equal Pay Act 1970 and Sex Discrimination Act 1975. It may also be able to help with advice and financial aid in taking a case through an Industrial Tribunal.

As well as helping with individual problems, the EOC campaigns for groups of people who may be denied equality of opportunity because of their sex. In addition to conducting research, it advises Parliament, employers, trade unions, education authorities and other organisations on how to promote equality. There is a Library and Information Centre at its Manchester headquarters, which has a wealth of material on this subject. It produces leaflets and books (many of which are free), plus posters, video tapes and films – a catalogue of these is available on request.

For further information, contact:

Equal Opportunities Commission, Overseas House, Quay Street, Manchester M3 3HN; tel 061-833 9244

Welsh Regional Office: Caerwys House, Windsor Lane, Cardiff CF1 1LB; tel 0222 43552

Scottish Regional Office: 141 West Nile Street, Glasgow G1 2RN; tel 041-332 8018

Press and media enquiries: 53 Poland Street, W1V 3DF; tel 071-287 3953

## The Industrial Society

The Industrial Society was formed over 70 years ago and works to develop the full use of the talents and potential of people at work, or seeking work, and to increase employee involvement and personal fulfilment through work. It is an independent, self-financing organisation with charitable status, and was granted its Royal charter in 1984.

The Secretarial Development Campaign was started in the 1960s to encourage both managers and secretaries to develop the working partnership to the full. Courses of up to three days are run regularly throughout the UK: a structure of five public courses offers secretaries at every level training in such things as administrative, presentation and communication skills, time management, managing change, assertiveness and stress management. For those supervising others, the skills of delegation, motivation, leadership and team-building, and interviewing techniques are among the topics covered. Managers are offered a seminar on how best to work with a secretary, and can also attend part of a course, with their secretary, to solve common work problems. Organisations generally sponsor delegates, and courses cost in the region of £400.

In the field of information technology, 'Proof-reading for word processing', a one-day course, offers help in this area to secretaries and other word processing users. The cost is round £200.

For further details, contact:

Secretarial Development Department, The Industrial Society, Peter Runge House, 3 Carlton House Terrace, London SW1 5DG; tel 071-839 4300

Information Technology Unit, The Industrial Society, Quadrant Court, 49 Calthorpe Road, Edgbaston, Birmingham B15 1TH; tel 021-454 6769.

The Industrial Society, Wira House, Clayton Wood Rise, Leeds LS16 6RF; tel 0532 780521

The Industrial Society, 4 West Regent Street, Glasgow G2 1RW; tel 041-332 2827

## Advisory, Conciliation and Arbitration Service (ACAS)

ACAS is an independent body whose regional enquiry points give free information to individuals on employment legislation, personnel and industrial relations matters. Requests for very detailed information are passed to a specialist advisory officer. However, ACAS do not give legal advice and will usually suggest that such enquiries are directed to a solicitor.

A current list of publications can be found in the back cover of 'This is ACAS', a free descriptive leaflet. Most are free and can be obtained from any ACAS office.

For further details contact:

ACAS, Head Office, 27 Wilton Street, London, SW1X 7AZ; tel 071-210 3000; fax 071-210 3708

Northern Region: Westgate House, Westgate Road, Newcastle upon Tyne NE1 1TJ; tel 091-261 2191; fax 091-232 5452

Yorkshire and Humberside: Commerce House, St Albans Place, Leeds LS2 8HH; tel 0532 431371; fax 0532 446678

London Region: Clifton House, 83–117 Euston Road, London NW1 2RB; tel 071-388 5100; fax 071-388 9722

South East Region: Westminster House, Fleet Road, Fleet, Hants GU13 8PD; tel 0252 811868; fax 0252 617006

South West Region: 27a Regent Street, Clifton, Bristol BS8 4HR; tel 0272 744066; fax 0272 744078

Midlands Region: Leonard House, 319–323 Bradford Street, Birmingham B5 6ET; tel 021-622 5050; fax 021-622 2244

Nottingham Office: Anderson House, Clinton Avenue, Nottingham NG5 1AW; tel 0602 693355; fax 0602 693085

North West Region: Boulton House, 17–21 Chorlton Street, Manchester M1 3HY; tel 061-228 3222; fax 061-228 7975

Merseyside Office: Cressington House, 249 St Mary's Road, Garston, Liverpool L19 0NF; tel 051-427 8881; fax 051-427 2715

Lancashire Office: Bradshawgate House, 1 Oak Street, Accrington BB5 1EQ; tel 0254 871996; fax 0254 383348

Scotland: Franborough House, 123–157 Bothwell Street, Glasgow G2 7JR; tel 041-204 2677; fax 041-221 4697

Wales: Phase 1, Ty Glas Road, Llanishen, Cardiff CF4 5PH; tel 0222 762636; fax 0222 751334

## Implications of the Single European Market

At the end of 1992 the Single European Market (SEM) will come into being with the removal of any physical, technical or fiscal barriers to trade between European Community (EC) states. This will have important consequences for working people who will need to know about conditions of employment, social security, training and rights of settlement in other EC states.

An excellent information pack on the SEM and its implications for employment, finance, families, equalities, law, trade unions and health can be obtained from City Centre. Written by Rohan Collier and entitled *1992 and You: The Impact of the Single European Market on Office Workers*, the pack costs £4 and can be obtained from City Centre at 32–35 Featherstone Street, London EC1Y 8QX: tel 071-608 1338. The brief outline of employment implications which follows relies heavily on information derived from this package.

The Single European Act came into force in 1987 and it provides the legal framework for achieving the Single European Market by December 1992. Competition from Japan and the USA has been the driving force behind the SEM. By the end of 1992 goods, capital, people and services will be able to move freely throughout the Community. Frontier controls between EC states will go, regulations about products and services will be removed, as will taxes on goods crossing borders. This is expected to result in less duplication of research and improved production of goods by making life easier for business and trade.

The SEM will bring about huge changes for people living within the EC. The free movement of people is one consequence of a frontier-free Europe. In 1989 2 million workers and 5 million EC nationals lived in an EC state that was not their own. This figure will increase following the SEM. Most of the legislation to implement the SEM has concentrated on the economic necessities. Little has been done on the social impact of 1992, apart from issues of health and safety at work.

With the SEM the EC will also be moving towards economic and monetary union. Most states have joined the ERM (Exchange Rate Mechanism) and the ECU (European Currency Unit) may eventually be the European currency.

## Employment

1992 will bring about huge changes in employment. At present there is high unemployment in Europe, with approximately 15 million people out of work across the Community. 1992 itself is expected to bring about 2 million new jobs at least. It will also provide the opportunity to work anywhere within the EC.

For office workers jobs in computing, telecommunications and equipment are likely to suffer; jobs in the finance sector, on the other hand, are likely to increase. The SEM will also bring about a shift towards white collar work – good news for secretaries.

## Looking for work in the EC

If you are an EC member (for example if you are British) you are already entitled to look for work in any EC state. There are still some formalities in Spain and Portugal but these will disappear by 1993. For secretarial work you would normally be expected to be fairly fluent in the local language – and English-speaking secretaries are likely to be in great demand throughout Europe from 1992 onwards.

If you find a job, you and your family will have right of residency in that country. However, you will have to get a resident's permit which will be valid for five years and is renewable on request. 'Family' includes: your spouse, children under 21, grandchildren under 21, children and grandchildren over 21 if they are still dependent on you, your parents and grandparents, and those of your spouse. All these members of your family are entitled to training and to look for work. This applies whether they are themselves EC members or not.

You and your family will be entitled to the same allowances, grants, maternity benefit, housing benefit and other benefits as nationals of the country in which you work. You will also be entitled to sickness benefit and a pension. You will have the right to retire and benefit from local facilities and allowances for pensioners – in any country you have worked.

### Pay and conditions after 1992
Many jobs pay more in other EC countries since most have minimum earnings legislation. France, Spain, Holland, Portugal and Luxembourg have minimum wage legislation. Belgium and Greece have national agreements on minimum pay negotiated between unions and employers which have the force of law. Italy, Germany and Denmark have widespread collective negotiated minimum rates of pay. The UK alone has virtually no legislation or national negotiated agreements on minimum pay.

On average workers are paid most in Denmark, followed by Germany, then in decreasing order of pay Holland, Belgium, Ireland, Britain, Italy, France and Spain, with Greece and Portugal right at the bottom. There are no laws planned by the EC on pay, despite the Social Charter saying that 'a decent wage shall be established'. The Commission will simply issue an 'option' on pay, probably with recommended minimum wages.

### Hours of work
Most EC states have legislation limiting weekly working hours, usually to something between 40 and 48 hours. Collective agreements have improved on this in most countries. The legal limit is:

- 48 hours in Germany, Italy, the Netherlands, Portugal and Ireland, but in fact collective agreements bring the average working week down to much less than this;

- 40 hours in Spain, Belgium, Greece and Luxembourg;
- 39 hours in France.

There is an EC proposal for legislation on working time in the Action Programme implementing the Social Charter which would give 'a maximum duration of work, rest periods, holidays, night work, weekend work and systematic overtime'. The maximum will probably be 40 hours, combined with flexibility to allow working time to be calculated over a longer period than a week.

Most countries have a statutory limit on overtime usually around two hours a day with a maximum in any one year. Denmark and Italy do not have anything in law but they have widespread collective agreements which are legally binding. Only the UK has no legal limit. The EC limit will probably be two hours per day.

## Holidays and weekly days of rest

The UK is the only EC state where holidays and a weekly day of rest are not guaranteed by law. Most countries have Sunday as the day of rest, or if work is done on a Sunday, the employer is legally obliged to provide another day of rest. France, Spain and Denmark have a legal requirement to provide 30 days' holiday a year; Germany 18. Negotiated agreements have resulted in most countries having more than the legal minimum.

- 5-6 weeks' annual leave is the average in Germany, France and Luxembourg;
- 5 weeks is the average in Denmark and Belgium;
- $4\frac{1}{2}$-5 weeks is the average in Portugal and Spain;
- 4-6 weeks in Italy and the UK;
- 4 weeks in Greece and Ireland.

The EC legal requirement will probably be for four weeks' leave annually and one day of rest in every seven.

## Qualifications

A directive planned for 1991 will give mutual recognition to professional qualifications given after at least three years' training. For skilled workers mutual recognition will be agreed. The TUC keeps a list of which qualifications are recognised in the EC in the run-up to 1992 and beyond, and they can also be contacted for advice at Congress House, Great Russell Street, London WC1B 3LS; tel 071-636 4030.

## Equal pay

Throughout Europe women earn less than men for work of equal value.

On average women earn two-thirds of the average male wage. The difference in earnings is larger in the UK than any other EC state at an equal stage of economic development. To address this issue the EC brought in a directive on equal pay which has the force of law in all EC states.

## Taxation

Taxation, inasmuch as it concerns personal income tax, is one area where there is no EC legislation and none is planned. The same is true for social insurance contributions (NI in the UK). Both remain instruments of a country's national economic policy objectives. How income tax is collected and how much is levied is up to each state to decide. However, in all countries of the EC progressive taxation exists with a sliding scale in which successive income bands are taxed at increasing rates. The deduction rate for social insurance contributions is fairly similar across the EC, with the exception of Spain and the UK where deductions are far less.

## Pensions

After 1993 no country within the EC will be able to discriminate against women on occupational pensions (the age at which the pension is given should be the same as well as the amount of money given). Pensionable age (when you start drawing your pension) is not the same as retirement age (when you stop work). Both are covered by the new legislation and discrimination will be illegal after 1993. At present equal pensionable age already exists in Denmark, France, Ireland, the Netherlands, Spain, Germany and Luxembourg.

Your pension is payable in any EC state regardless of where your insurance was paid. The only exception to this are pensions from the Civil Service which are paid only in the UK.

If your insurance period in one EC state is not long enough to entitle you to a state pension under the laws of that country, the insurance periods gained in other EC states will be taken into account. Each country then grants you a proportion of the pension corresponding to the period for which you were actually insured in that state. Qualification periods for state pensions vary too, from three years' residence in Denmark, 60 months of insurance contributions in Germany, and 4050 working days contributions in Greece! Pensionable ages vary too; for example, they vary from 60 in France to 67 in Denmark.

If you leave your job to work abroad, you will lose part of your pension in the same way as if you change jobs within Britain. However, as more and more people will move around and work abroad for part of their lives, employers will have to consider providing occupational pensions on a Europe wide basis.

## Unemployment benefit

In all EC states unemployment benefit depends on a certain number of insurance contributions having been paid (there are some differences from one country to the next – for example, some pay benefits to school leavers looking for work). Contributions paid in one country can be added on to contributions paid in another in order to qualify for unemployment benefit. All require that you be fit for work, available for work and signing on at an unemployment office.

If you are without work and want to look for work in another EC state, you can claim unemployment benefit from that state for up to three months so long as:

- You would be entitled to unemployment benefit in the UK;
- You have been looking for work for at least four weeks in the UK prior to going abroad;
- You register with the unemployment office in the state in which you are looking for work;
- You are in possession of form E303 – available from the DSS or unemployment offices in the UK.

As a rule unemployment benefit is higher in other EC states.

## Family or child benefit

You can claim family allowances (child benefit) in any EC state. Family allowances are paid for children, adopted children, stepchildren and other children in your care. The age limit varies from country to country. In some it is children under 18 (in the UK if they are in full-time education), others pay for children up to age 25 if they are in full-time higher education (Belgium, Luxembourg, Portugal), some even up to age 27 (Germany, the Netherlands). In all countries there is no age limit for children with disabilities.

Amounts vary enormously; sometimes they are dependent on the parents' income. In many countries the first child receives different amounts from the second, third, and so on. The rules are complicated and vary from time to time. You need to take advice from your local DSS (local to the country in which you live).

## Protection of pregnant women

This directive (still in draft form at the time of writing) would impose legal requirements on all EC states. The proposals include:

- The right to 14 weeks' maternity leave on full pay.
- Protection against dismissal on grounds of pregnancy;

170

- Two weeks' leave immediately before the expected date of confinement;
- Paid leave for ante-natal examinations;
- A requirement for employers to reorganise the working conditions and hours of pregnant women to protect their health and safety;
- A protection for pregnant women against specified harmful industrial agents (toxic materials), processes or other risks;
- A requirement that an alternative to night-time work be made available to pregnant night workers for a period of at least 16 weeks before and after the birth.

If this directive comes into force women will qualify for all of these so long as they are in work or registered unemployed from the beginning of their pregnancy. This is quite different from present UK law, where women only qualify for maternity rights after two years' full-time (or 5 years part-time) employment.

City Centre's excellent information pack on the impact of 1992 contains information on current maternity rights in the EC with country-by-country comparisons of maternity leave, parental leave, childcare facilities (pre- and school age), time off for sick children and care of the elderly.

**Further information**
City Centre's '1992' pack (see page 146 for address) includes information on:

- Health care in the EC;
- Health and safety at work;
- Sexual harassment;
- Equality (women, race, disability, age);
- EC legal framework;
- Recourse to European law;
- EC legislation;
- Legal rights after 1992;
- Trade unions;
- Help and resources (including a list of further reading).

in addition to more extensive information on living and working in the EC after 1993.

# Acknowledgements

This book would not have been completed without the help and kindness of many people. I should like to thank all those who have been involved, and especially:

Staff at the Department of Employment/Work Research Unit Libraries
Corinne Devery and Juliet Hepburn, The Industrial Society
Siobhan Hamilton-Phillips, Vocational Guidance Association
Helen Holden, Equal Opportunities Commission
Tim Birchinall, Times Newspapers Ltd
Christine Little, Federation of Recruitment & Employment Services Ltd
Angela Paterson, Trusthouse Forte plc
Annie Sutcliffe and Nicollette Agnew, Crone Corkill & Associates
Patricia Moore, British Tourist Authority
Alison Vickers, National Council for Civil Liberties
Wendy Syer, Abbey National plc
Peter Worger, Association of Conference Executives
Alan Niblett, Central Statistics Office
Jane Hall, The Information Bureau
Bernard McDonnell, ACAS
Doreen Huntley

# Index